The Fashionable Cocktail

The Fashionable Cocktail

200 Fabulous Drinks for the Fashion Set

JANE ROCCA

Illustrations by Neryl Walker

hardie grant books

MELBOURNE · LONDON

Contents

Glass types

Boston A boston cocktail shaker is used when mixing drinks, is made of glass and metal and is pretty much all you need when making cocktails in your kitchen. You can serve the cocktail in the glass part of the shaker.

Brandy snifter Also known as a brandy balloon or cognac glass, this wide-based and narrow-topped glass is – you guessed it – popular for brandy drinks and those with complex notes.

Champagne flute It's your go-to glass for all things bubbly. It's a tall-stemmed glass to enjoy Champagne and other sparkling wines in.

Claret This is a medium-sized wine glass, often used for white wine and popular for cocktails, too.

Colada Rum-based cocktails always lean towards the colada glass. It looks like it belongs beside a pool or beach – don't you agree?

Collins/tumbler Collins is a fancy way of saying tumbler; but remember, it's more narrow.

Coupette/coupe This is a larger and rounder version of a cocktail glass. It favours salty rims and is also used for daiquiris.

 Highball A glass tumbler used to serve mixed drinks, and ideal for light spirits.

Hurricane A tall and elegant glass named for its resemblance to a hurricane lamp. Exotic cocktails are well-suited drinks.

 Jam jar Yep, as the name suggests – keep those jam jars handy as they will be required for making modern cocktails. We love the rustic wide-bellied ones for a Nanna touch.

Julep cup This is a pewter cup – a fancy way of serving cocktails, which requires you to hold the cup by its bottom or top edge to allow keeping the drink cooler for longer.

 Mason jar Think of a preserving jar and that's exactly what you need here.

Martini Sometimes referred to as a cocktail glass, the martini is a triangle bowl design with a long stem. It is used for a wide range of straight-up-without-ice cocktails. There is a shorter version, too.

 Metal camping mug It doesn't get more rustic than this mug built for outdoor adventures. But the camping mug is now kitsch in the cocktail world and perfect for hearty drinking moments.

Old-fashioned/rocks/lowball So many various ways to describe the same thing – just remember, this glass is a short round glass suitable for drinks served on the rocks. It typically has a thick base and is perfect for muddling ingredients in.

Poco Used for fancy cocktails and any layered drink. Looks a bit like the colada.

Punch cup Head to your mother's 'best' cupboards for optimal punch cup finds.

Shot Usually used for straight booze and, yes, for cocktails drunk in one fell swoop.

Sling Usually reserved for long drinks served with ice.

Small pitcher Again, a small glass pitcher is what you're after for an eclectic approach to barware.

Stemless wine It's easy to hold and is a modern take on wine glasses, and sometimes doubles as a tumbler.

Whisky It's a smaller version of a tumbler and usually reserved for whisky based-tipples.

Wine Used to serve wine or port. You decide.

Notes

Sugar syrup

To make sugar syrup, the ratio is always 1 part water to 2 parts sugar. Place 250 ml (8½ fl oz/1 cup) water in a saucepan over medium heat and bring to the boil. Add 440 g (15½ oz/2 cups) white sugar and stir until it dissolves. Remove from the heat immediately and allow to cool before using.

Vanilla sugar syrup

Follow the recipe above for sugar syrup and then add a few drops of vanilla extract to the sugar syrup for a gentle vanilla infusion.

Spice syrup

Place 250 ml (8½ fl oz/1 cup) water, 460 g (1 lb/2 cups) firmly packed brown sugar, 2 cinnamon sticks, 1 clove, 1 teaspoon freshly grated nutmeg, 1 teaspoon allspice and 1 tablespoon grated orange zest in a saucepan. Bring to the boil and stir until the sugar is dissolved. Remove from the heat immediately, allow to cool, strain and bottle.

The Vintage Girl

The vintage girl is positively hung up on the past. Her wardrobe is beaming with dresses under the spell of a different time. She treasures gowns that waltzed in the wee hours of somebody else's late-night rendezvous, and adores her sequinned party dresses because they whiff of dreams and hopes from another era. She's a collector of fine couture that's perfectly intact despite its age.

She's the sort of girl who doesn't fall for fads either – she's all about keeping her clock ticking to a classic time. She likes to dream a little and dance a lot and, when it comes to drinking, the vintage girl will cling to the classics – those tipples that conjure the smells of old-school dance halls, jazz clubs and stylish, velvet-lavished drinking locales.

She's the one who mixes and matches her wardrobe with quality vintage finds, and borrows from style icons of the past to channel the '50s with pin-up austerity in mind, or might choose to swing with the '60s – footnoting fashion's giant leap into mod-style lengths and geometric patterns – or even embrace the hippie era of the '70s. The vintage girl is all about taking the best of what's come before and proving that vintage isn't passé – it's her rite of passage and here to stay.

Old-Fashioned

1 sugar cube
3 dashes of bitters
2 orange slices
60 ml (2 fl oz/¼ cup) Irish whiskey
maraschino cherry to garnish

Place a sugar cube in an old-fashioned glass
and saturate with the bitters. Add 1 orange
slice and muddle the ingredients. Fill the
glass with ice and add the whiskey. Stir well.
Garnish with the second orange slice and
the maraschino cherry.

Old-fashioned

Debutante

2 dashes of orange bitters
25 ml (¾ fl oz) fresh lime juice
25 ml (¾ fl oz) grenadine
60 ml (2 fl oz/¼ cup) gin
lime wedge to garnish

Shake all the ingredients with ice and strain
into a chilled coupette glass. Garnish with a
lime wedge.

Coupette

Eastside Cocktail

4 mint leaves
30 ml (1 fl oz) fresh lime juice
25 ml (¾ fl oz) sugar syrup (see page 9)
60 ml (2 fl oz/¼ cup) gin
cucumber slice to garnish

Shake all the ingredients with ice and strain into
a chilled martini glass. Garnish with a cucumber
slice on the rim.

Martini

Perfect Lady

1 egg white
15 ml (½ fl oz) fresh lemon juice
30 ml (1 fl oz) apricot liqueur
45 ml (1½ fl oz) gin

Dry-shake all the ingredients, without ice, to emulsify, then shake vigorously with ice. Strain into a large coupette glass.

Coupette

Peach Bellini

SERVES 8

2–3 ripe refrigerated peaches
1 bottle Tempus Two Pewter
   Sparkling Pinot Noir Chardonnay

Use a blender to purée the peaches.
Put 2 tablespoons of the purée in the
base of each chilled Champagne flute.
Pour over the chilled Tempus Two Pewter
Sparkling.

Champagne

Amelia

15 ml (½ fl oz) sugar syrup (see page 9)
45 ml (1½ fl oz) Eristoff vodka
15 ml (½ fl oz) St Germain elderflower liqueur
30 ml (1 fl oz) blueberry purée
20 ml (⅔ fl oz) fresh lemon juice
30 ml (1 fl oz) apple juice
8 mint leaves
3 dashes of Regans' Orange Bitters

Shake all the ingredients with ice and fine-strain into a chilled martini glass.

Martini

A Christmas Cocktail

5 fresh cranberries
3 rosemary sprigs
90 ml (3 fl oz) Hendrick's gin
60 ml (2 fl oz/¼ cup) cranberry juice

Lightly muddle the cranberries and rosemary sprigs in a glass, leaving them somewhat intact, then add them to a chilled martini glass. In a shaker of ice, add the gin and cranberry juice. Shake and strain into the martini glass over the cranberries and rosemary.

Martini

Blood Orange Aperitivo

30 ml (1 fl oz) gin
30 ml (1 fl oz) Aperol
juice of ½ blood orange

Shake all the ingredients with ice and strain into a martini glass.

Martini

Femme Fatale

40 ml (1⅓ fl oz) Pama pomegranate liqueur
20 ml (⅔ fl oz) Disaronno amaretto
30 ml (1 fl oz) fresh lemon juice
1 barspoon caster (superfine) sugar
1 egg white
3 drops of Fee Brothers Bitters
flamed orange peel to garnish (see method)

Put all the ingredients into a shaker. Shake hard with ice and double-strain into a martini glass. Garnish with the flamed orange peel.

(To make the flamed orange peel, hold a match flame to the skin side of the orange peel until it burns slightly.)

Martini

Henry M Jones

yellow Chartreuse dust to rim glass
  (see method)
30 ml (1 fl oz) Hennessy VS cognac
30 ml (1 fl oz) Cointreau
10 ml (⅓ fl oz) Joseph Cartron crème
  de peche
30 ml (1 fl oz) fresh lemon juice

To make the Chartreuse dust,
pour a whole bottle of Chartreuse
into a large baking tray and sit it
elevated in a warm environment
until the liquid evaporates (3–4
days). All that will be left is a
crusty layer. Crush this layer in
a spice blender.

To make the cocktail, dust
the rim of the glass with the
yellow Chartreuse. Shake all the
ingredients with ice and fine-
strain into a martini glass.

Martini

La Margarita Damiana

rock salt to lace mug
30 ml (1 fl oz) Espolòn Reposado tequila
30 ml (1 fl oz) Damiana
splash of organic agave syrup
60 ml (2 fl oz/¼ cup) fresh lime juice
30 ml (1 fl oz) fresh lemon juice

Lace one side of a chilled metal camping
mug with rock salt. Shake all the remaining
ingredients vigorously with large ice cubes.
Pour into a chilled metal camping mug.

Metal camping mug

Americano

 30 ml (1 fl oz) Campari
30 ml (1 fl oz) sweet vermouth
soda water (club soda)
orange slice to garnish

Pour the Campari and vermouth over ice in an old-fashioned glass. Top with soda water and garnish with an orange slice.

Old-fashioned

The Jukebox Jodi

7 raspberries
3 mint leaves
60 ml (2 fl oz/¼ cup) pineapple-infused white rum (see method)
Champagne or Prosecco
splash of pineapple juice
wedge of pineapple and a raspberry threaded onto
  a cocktail umbrella to garnish

To infuse the white rum with pineapple, cut ¼ fresh pineapple
into small chunks, without skin, and let stand in 1 litre
(34 fl oz/4 cups) white rum for at least 24 hours.

To make the cocktail, muddle 5 raspberries and the mint leaves in
a large brandy snifter. Shake the pineapple-infused white rum with
ice. Strain the rum into the snifter over the berries and mint, then
top with Champagne or Prosecco and garnish with the remaining
2 raspberries. Add the pineapple juice. Garnish with the wedge of
pineapple and raspberry on a cocktail umbrella.

Brandy snifter

Grapefruit Collins

2 dashes of Peychaud's bitters
15 ml (½ fl oz) fresh lemon juice
15 ml (½ fl oz) sugar syrup (see page 9)
45 ml (1½ fl oz) pink grapefruit juice
60 ml (2 fl oz/¼ cup) gin
soda water (club soda)
grapefruit slice to garnish

Shake and strain all the ingredients, except the soda water, into a highball glass with ice. Top with soda water and garnish with the grapefruit slice.

Highball

Number 5

45 ml (1½ fl oz) Don Julio Blanco tequila
15 ml (½ fl oz) St Germain elderflower liqueur
15 ml (½ fl oz) fresh lemon juice
1 dash of peach bitters
grapefruit foam (see method) and grapefruit twist to garnish

To make the grapefruit foam, place 1 tablespoon sugar, 1 tablespoon fresh grapefruit juice and an egg white in a whipped cream charger. Shake and spray.

To make the cocktail, shake all the ingredients with ice and fine-strain into a coupette glass. Layer the grapefruit foam on top. Garnish with the grapefruit twist.

Coupette

Sugar Daddy

45 ml (1½ fl oz) Sailor Jerry rum
15 ml (½ fl oz) Tuaca vanilla citrus liqueur
1 whole egg
2 dashes of chocolate bitters
10 ml (⅓ fl oz) vanilla sugar syrup (see page 9)
freshly grated nutmeg to garnish

Dry-shake all the ingredients, then shake again
with ice and strain into a wine glass. Garnish
with nutmeg.

Wine

Voiron Gold

20 ml (⅔ fl oz) tequila blanco
20 ml (⅔ fl oz) yellow Chartreuse
20 ml (⅔ fl oz) fresh lime juice
15 ml (½ fl oz) Frangelico
5 ml (¼ fl oz) sugar syrup (see page 9)

Add all the ingredients to a shaker.
Shake with ice and double-strain
into a coupette glass.

Coupette

La Vida

¼ green apple
1 barspoon caster (superfine) sugar
30 ml (1 fl oz) Sauvignon Blanc
30 ml (1 fl oz) Tanqueray gin
20 ml (⅔ fl oz) Zubrówka Bison Grass vodka
10 ml (⅓ fl oz) Tuaca vanilla citrus liqueur
3 basil leaves, plus extra to garnish

Muddle the apple and caster sugar in a Boston shaker.
Add the Sauvignon Blanc, gin, vodka and Tuaca. Add the basil
leaves and shake with ice. Double-strain into a chilled martini
glass and garnish with a floating basil leaf.

Martini

Cucumber Collins

45 ml (1½ fl oz) Hendrick's gin
15 ml (½ fl oz) Limoncello
30 ml (1 fl oz) cucumber purée
20 ml (⅔ fl oz) fresh lemon juice
10 ml (⅓ fl oz) sugar syrup (see page 9)
soda water (club soda)
cucumber stick to garnish

Build the cocktail in a highball glass with ice and top with soda water. Garnish with a cucumber stick.

Highball

Tom Collins

60 ml (2 fl oz/¼ cup) gin
30 ml (1 fl oz) fresh lemon juice
30 ml (1 fl oz) sugar syrup (see page 9)
soda water (club soda)
lemon slice and maraschino cherry to garnish

Fill a cocktail shaker with ice. Pour in the gin,
lemon juice and sugar syrup. Shake and strain
into a highball glass with ice. Top with soda
water and garnish with a lemon slice and
a maraschino cherry.

Highball

Fresh Fig Manhattan

1 large fresh fig
15 ml (½ fl oz) sweet vermouth
2 dashes of angostura bitters
60 ml (2 fl oz/¼ cup) Old Overholt Straight
   Rye Whiskey
sliver of fig to garnish

Muddle the whole fig with the vermouth. In a
shaker of ice add the bitters and whiskey. Shake
to oblivion and strain into a chilled martini glass.
Add a sliver of fig to float on top.

Martini

Turkish Delight Martini

30 ml (1 fl oz) 666 Pure Tasmanian Vodka
30 ml (1 fl oz) Ketel One Citroen
15 ml (½ fl oz) Bols cacao white
15 ml (½ fl oz) fresh lemon juice
15 ml (½ fl oz) cranberry juice
rose petal to garnish

Shake all the ingredients with ice and pour
into a martini glass. Garnish with a rose petal.

Martini

Number 4

50 ml (1⅔ fl oz) Belvedere Black Raspberry
  vodka
20 ml (⅔ fl oz) clarified lemon juice
15 ml (½ fl oz) Monin Violette violet liqueur
orchid to garnish

⌐

Shake all the ingredients with ice and
fine-strain into a martini glass. Garnish
with an orchid.

Martini

Airmail

15 ml (½ fl oz) honey syrup (see method)
15 ml (½ fl oz) fresh lime juice
30 ml (1 fl oz) light rum
Champagne

⌐

To make the honey syrup, the ratio is
1 part water to 3 parts honey. Put the
honey and water in a pan and stir until
the honey dissolves. Gently bring to
the boil, then reduce heat and simmer,
stirring, until thickened. Remove from
the heat and allow to cool.

To make the cocktail, shake all the
ingredients, except the Champagne, with
ice and strain into a chilled Champagne
flute. Top with Champagne.

Champagne

Cucumber Southside

45 ml (1½ fl oz) Hendrick's gin
25 ml (¾ fl oz) fresh lime juice
15 ml (½ fl oz) sugar syrup (see page 9)
muddled cucumber and a handful of mint leaves
   to garnish

Shake all the ingredients with ice and strain into a
martini glass. Float the cucumber in the glass and
garnish with mint.

Martini

The Season
Chaser

The season chaser* is the most organised girl of all. Her wardrobe is categorised according to seasonal moods and textural shifts in the fabrics she wears. If her outfits were dotted on an airport runway, they would light up the tarmac, always ready to take her to some new and exotic corner of the world.

Just as her taste in fashion is plotted according to seasons, so too is her palette of cocktails. Whether she's chasing the catwalks of Paris, London, New York or Milan, she uses the same instinct to season her own drinking urge. And when it comes to her cocktails, she's a lover of experimentation, from pretty flower-soaked liqueurs to muddled fruits and flavoured spirits. She's all about building a drink to match her style – a drop of this, a dash of that. Whether her drinks are chilli chocolate–soaked for winter flings or flutes brimming with Champagne and rum for summery toasts, she'll be the one raising a glass no matter what axis she's spinning on.

The seasonal gal embraces the vibrancy of spring, gets wrapped in the knits of winter yet, come autumn, she's all about turning over a new leaf. She's the moon chaser, the sun follower, the eclipse lover – but deep down she's the one you'll spot chasing a fashionable party regardless of what's happening with the weather.

Strawberry & Basil Fields

60 ml (2 fl oz/¼ cup) strawberry and basil purée (see method)
45 ml (1½ fl oz) vodka
15 ml (½ fl oz) strawberry liqueur
15 ml (½ fl oz) fresh lemon juice
30 ml (1 fl oz) apple juice
30 ml (1 fl oz) cranberry juice

To make the strawberry and basil purée, process 250 g (9 oz) strawberries and 9 basil leaves in a blender.

To make the cocktail, shake all the ingredients with ice and pour over crushed ice in a collins glass.

Collins

La Paloma

20 ml (⅔ fl oz) Tromba blanco tequila
splash of organic agave syrup
pinch of salt
small splash of fresh lime juice
90 ml (3 fl oz) fresh pink grapefruit juice
Jarritos Toronja Mexican soda
wedge of pink grapefruit to garnish

Shake all the ingredients, except the soda, with
ice in a large mason jar. Top with the soda and
garnish with a wedge of pink grapefruit. Serve in
the jar.

Large mason jar

Hendrick's Mojito

45 ml (1½ fl oz) Hendrick's gin
20 ml (⅔ fl oz) fresh lime juice
15 ml (½ fl oz) sugar syrup (see page 9)
mint leaves
2–3 muddled limes
soda water (club soda)

Build the cocktail in a collins glass with crushed ice and top with soda water.

Collins

Rhubarb Custard

45 ml (1½ fl oz) rhubarb purée (see method)
30 ml (1 fl oz) sloe gin
30 ml (1 fl oz) vanilla vodka
15 ml (½ fl oz) fresh lemon juice
60 ml (2 fl oz/¼ cup) cloudy apple juice

To make the rhubarb purée, place 2 chopped
stalks rhubarb, 140 g (5 oz/⅔ cup) sugar and
60 ml (2 fl oz/¼ cup) water in a saucepan and
cook over low heat for 25 minutes. Process in a
blender until smooth. Cool before using.

To make the cocktail, shake and pour
all the ingredients over ice cubes
in a collins glass.

Collins

Chef's Bite

45 ml (1½ fl oz) gin
15 ml (½ fl oz) Boulard Grand
   Solage calvados

15 ml (½ fl oz) lime juice cordial
lime twist to garnish

Shake all the ingredients with ice
and strain into an old-fashioned
glass. Garnish with a lime twist.

Old-fashioned

Spring Fling

5 mm (¼ in) cucumber wedge
3 drops of rosewater
1 barspoon mixed berries (blackberries,
   raspberries and blueberries)
15 ml (½ fl oz) sugar syrup (see page 9)
50 ml (1⅔ fl oz) Hendrick's gin
30 ml (1 fl oz) fresh lemon juice
5 ml (¼ fl oz) crème de mure or Chambord
lemon wedge to garnish

Muddle the cucumber and rosewater in
a Boston shaker. Add the berries, sugar
syrup and the remaining ingredients,
except the crème de mure. Shake and
strain over ice into an old-fashioned
glass. Float the crème de mure on top
and garnish with a lemon wedge.

Old-fashioned

Apple Garden

50 ml (1⅔ fl oz) vodka
30 ml (1 fl oz) De Kuyper Sour Apple Pucker
15 ml (½ fl oz) butterscotch schnapps
15 ml (½ fl oz) apple juice
slice of green apple to garnish

Shake all the ingredients with ice and strain into a martini glass. Garnish with a slice of green apple.

Martini

Chilli Chocolate Martini

5 dashes of chilli tincture (see method)
30 ml (1 fl oz) espresso coffee
30 ml (1 fl oz) Mount Gay rum
30 ml (1 fl oz) Averna
15 ml (½ fl oz) Monin white chocolate syrup
4 dashes of chocolate bitters
coffee beans to garnish

To make the chilli tincture, cover
2–3 chillies with Mount Gay rum for
2 weeks then strain.

To make the cocktail, shake all the
ingredients with ice and strain into a
martini glass. Garnish with coffee beans.

Martini

White Chocolate Espresso Martini

finely grated white chocolate to dust rim
30 ml (1 fl oz) vanilla vodka
30 ml (1 fl oz) Mozart white chocolate liqueur
20 ml (⅔ fl oz) Monin white chocolate syrup
30 ml (1 fl oz) espresso coffee

Dust half the rim of a martini glass with
finely grated white chocolate. Shake all
the ingredients with ice and strain into
the glass.

Martini

Truffle Airmail

honey to rim glass
truffle salt to rim glass
40 ml (1⅓ fl oz) Bacardi 151 rum
20 ml (⅔ fl oz) fresh lime juice
10 ml (⅓ fl oz) organic agave syrup
30 ml (1 fl oz) sparkling wine

Prepare the lip of a Champagne flute
with a thin rim of honey, allowing it
to run down the inside of the glass.
Sprinkle a liberal amount of truffle
salt on the rim. Place in the freezer
while you make the drink. Add all
the ingredients, except the sparkling
wine, to a shaker. Shake with ice and
double-strain into your prepared
glass. Top with the sparkling wine.

Champagne

Xanadu Fancy

20 ml (⅔ fl oz) passionfruit vodka
20 ml (⅔ fl oz) Aperol
20 ml (⅔ fl oz) cranberry juice
20 ml (⅔ fl oz) fresh lime juice
10 ml (⅓ fl oz) orgeat syrup
flamed orange peel to garnish (see method)

Add all the ingredients to a shaker.
Shake with ice and double-strain into
a martini glass. Garnish with flamed
orange peel.

(To make the flamed orange peel, hold
a match flame to the skin side of the
orange peel until it burns slightly.)

Martini

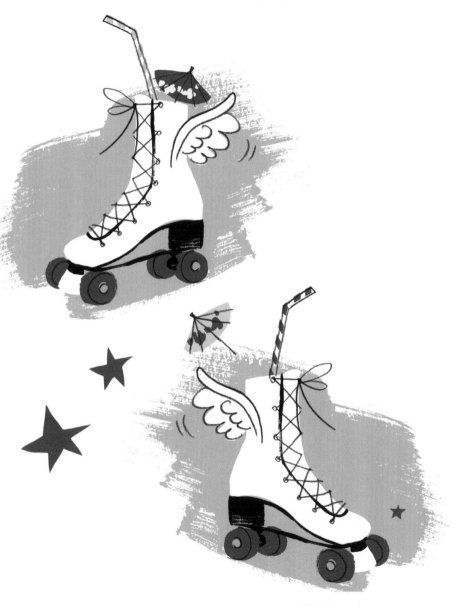

Blossoming Youth

45 ml (1½ fl oz) Hendrick's gin
15 ml (½ fl oz) St Germain elderflower liqueur
30 ml (1 fl oz) fresh lemon juice
15 ml (½ fl oz) sugar syrup (see page 9)
5 ml (¼ fl oz) crème de violette

Shake all the ingredients, except the crème de violette, with ice and double-strain into a coupette glass. Float the crème de violette on top.

Coupette

Tried & Tested

60 ml (2 fl oz/¼ cup) Ron Añejo Pampero Selección rum
10 ml (⅓ fl oz) cloudy apple juice
5 ml (¼ fl oz) cinnamon and clove syrup (see method)
1 dash of Fee Brothers Chocolate Bitters
1 dash of angostura bitters
1 pink lady apple fan with 5 cloves to garnish (see method)

To make the cinnamon and clove syrup, place 230 g (8 oz/1 cup) sugar, 250 ml (8½ fl oz/1 cup) water, 1 broken cinnamon stick and 1 tablespoon whole or ground cloves in a saucepan. Heat on high until the sugar dissolves. Remove from the heat and allow to cool. Strain the mixture through a piece of muslin (cheesecloth) to remove the cinnamon and cloves.

To make the apple fan, slice off one cheek of the apple. Place flat on a chopping board and cut 8 thin slices, but do not cut right through the apple. Fan the pieces out and stud the apple with 5 cloves along the top of the fan.

To make the cocktail, add 15 ml (½ fl oz) rum at a time, stirring for 5 seconds between pours, into an old-fashioned glass filled with ice. Pour in the cloudy apple juice and then add all the other ingredients. Finish with the apple fan. Place the fan on top of the ice, resting on the rim of the glass.

Old-fashioned

Hana Ocha Margarita

30 ml (1 fl oz) Herradura Reposado tequila
30 ml (1 fl oz) Zen green tea liqueur
15 ml (½ fl oz) elderflower cordial
10 ml (⅓ fl oz) fresh lemon juice
5 ml (¼ fl oz) yuzu juice

⌒

Add all the ingredients to a shaker with ice. Shake hard and double-strain into a martini glass.

Martini

The Impossible Sazerac

dash of absinthe to coat glass
55 ml (1¾ fl oz) 666 Pure Tasmanian Vodka
10 ml (⅓ fl oz) Ron Matusalem
   Blanco Platino rum
10 ml (⅓ fl oz) sugar syrup (see page 9)
dash of Peychaud's bitters

⌒

Coat a chilled old-fashioned glass with a dash of absinthe. Stir all the ingredients with ice in a mixing glass. When well chilled, strain into the old-fashioned glass.

Old-fashioned

The Blowout–Motor City

1 squirt of Worcestershire sauce
1 garlic clove or jalapeño-stuffed olive
90 ml (3 fl oz) chilled Absolut Peppar vodka

Put the Worcestershire sauce in the bottom
of a shot glass and place the garlic clove or
jalapeño-stuffed olive in the sauce. Pour the
vodka into the glass, shoot the shot and eat
the garlic clove or olive quickly.

Shot

Mad as a March Hare

45 ml (1½ fl oz) tea-infused 666 Autumn Butter Vodka (see method)
strawberry sugar to garnish (see method)
30 g (1 oz) strawberry jam
25 ml (¾ fl oz) fresh lemon juice

To make the tea-infused vodka, add 20 g (¾ oz) leaf tea to a bottle of
666 Autumn Butter Vodka. Set aside and agitate once a day for a week.
Strain out the tea leaves before using.

To make the strawberry sugar, mix together an equal amount of
dehydrated strawberries and caster (superfine) sugar.

To make the cocktail, rim a small punch cup with the strawberry sugar.
Add all the ingredients to a shaker with ice and shake vigorously. Double-
strain into the punch cup.

Small punch cup

Pacific Isle

30 ml (1 fl oz) white rum
30 ml (1 fl oz) Umeshu
30 ml (1 fl oz) yuzu liqueur
15 ml (½ fl oz) fresh lemon juice
15 ml (½ fl oz) sugar syrup (see page 9)
twist of lemon to garnish

Shake all the ingredients with ice and
strain into a martini glass. Garnish with
a twist of lemon.

Martini

White Chocolate & Passionfruit Martini

finely grated white chocolate to rim glass
30 ml (1 fl oz) vanilla vodka
15 ml (½ fl oz) Joseph Cartron fruit de la passion
15 ml (½ fl oz) fresh pink grapefruit juice
30 ml (1 fl oz) passionfruit purée
15 ml (½ fl oz) Monin white chocolate syrup
1 egg white

Rim a martini glass with finely grated white chocolate.
Dry-shake all the ingredients, then shake with ice
and strain into the glass.

Martini

Lost in Translation

20 ml (⅔ fl oz) Yamazaki 12-year-old whisky
15 ml (½ fl oz) caramel liqueur
10 ml (⅓ fl oz) chocolate syrup
10 ml (⅓ fl oz) vanilla-infused cream
dash of egg white
sarsaparilla
chocolate sprinkles to garnish

Stir all the ingredients, except the sarsaparilla, in a Boston
shaker and pour over ice cubes. Top up with sarsaparilla and
garnish with the chocolate sprinkles.

Boston

Nakatomi Towers

2 muddled apricots
45 ml (1½ fl oz) Shochu
30 ml (1 fl oz) yuzu juice
10 ml (⅓ fl oz) sugar syrup (see page 9)
lemonade

Build all the ingredients, except the lemonade, in
a Boston shaker with ice. Dry-shake the ingredients
and top up with crushed ice and lemonade.

Boston

Beast of Bourbon

45 ml (1½ fl oz) Jacquin's Rock & Rye
15 ml (½ fl oz) amaretto
20 ml (⅔ fl oz) cherry tea
80 ml (2½ fl oz/⅓ cup) Mandarine Napoléon
squeeze of fresh lime juice
5 ml (¼ fl oz) orgeat syrup
lime twist to garnish

Shake with ice cubes in a Boston shaker then
double-strain into the Boston glass. Garnish
with a lime twist.

Boston

The Sartorialist

The sartorialist femme is all about precision. She doesn't curate her look according to anybody's gospel but her own and, when it comes to measures, she's only interested in applying those to the world of cocktail-making and not her fashion sense. She's all about timeless appeal and classic wardrobe pieces that stand the test of time. She lives high atop fashion's very own cliff ready to take a giant leap of faith in her own uninhibited world of dress.

If fashion is fleeting, then the sartorialist woman is there to remind you that style is eternal. She prefers to travel in the fast lane – usually parked in the front row of fashion shows if her schedule allows (nudge, wink). As Giorgio Armani once said, elegance doesn't mean being noticed, it means being remembered. The sartorialist woman is about individualism. It's as much about what she's wearing at special occasions as it is about how she shuffles her outfits with no party to plan for. She takes sartorial risks, maps her own journey from gem finds and new fashion pieces, and rocks her look in her own way. She'd fit right in, in the streets of Paris, London or New York and a photographer would be there waiting to take her photo, and voyeurs planning to mimic her style.

When it comes to drinking, the sartorialist will don a blazer soaked in rum, a turkey wrapped in whisky and save honey for the monsoon season – she's a risk taker, a heartbreaker and lives by the motto: it's not what you drink, but how you drink it.

The Red Winds

20 ml (⅔ fl oz) red capsicum (bell pepper) purée
   (see method)
6 pieces salted cucumber (see method)
45 ml (1½ fl oz) The West Winds Cutlass gin
10 ml (⅓ fl oz) sugar syrup (see page 9)
15 ml (½ fl oz) fresh lemon juice
2 dashes of orange bitters
lemon twist to garnish

To make the red capsicum purée, process the flesh of
1 red capsicum in a blender.

To make the salted cucumber, peel a cucumber and
place the skins in lightly salted water. Allow to stand
for 30–45 minutes until softened.

To make the cocktail, mix all the ingredients in a Boston
shaker and shake vigorously with ice. Fine-strain into a
coupette glass. Garnish with a lemon twist.

Coupette

The Blue Cheese Olive Martini

MOTOR CITY BAR LES ORIGINAL

blue cheese olives (see method)
olive brine (the brine in which olives
  are pickled)
dry vermouth bianco
120 ml (4 fl oz) vodka

To make the blue cheese olives, stuff
green olives with blue cheese, cover
with brine and chill.

To make the cocktail, in a shaker of ice
add a splash of vermouth, the vodka
and a dash of olive brine. Shake and
pour into a chilled martini glass with the
blue cheese olives. (Always use an odd
number of olives or it's bad luck!)

Martini

Smashed Turkey

½ mandarin, skin left on
40 ml (1⅓ fl oz) Wild Turkey rye whiskey
15 ml (½ fl oz) Grand Marnier
20 ml (⅔ fl oz) fresh lemon juice
10 ml (⅓ fl oz) sugar syrup (see page 9)
8 mint leaves
wedge of mandarin and a large mint leaf
  to garnish

Muddle the mandarin in the bottom
of a Boston shaker. Add all the other
ingredients and shake hard with ice.
Strain into a large wine glass over fresh
ice cubes and garnish with the wedge
of mandarin and large mint leaf.

Wine

Black Blazer

30 ml (1 fl oz) Jamaican rum
15 ml (½ fl oz) dark overproof rum
2 dashes of aromatic bitters
10 ml (⅓ fl oz) dark chocolate liqueur
10 ml (⅓ fl oz) white chocolate syrup
1 small square of plain chocolate
lemon twist to garnish

Add 15 ml (½ fl oz) boiling water to a 2 litre (68 fl oz/8 cup) stainless steel pitcher. Add all the ingredients to a small glass. Place the glass inside the pitcher. Wait for the ingredients to heat up and the chocolate to melt. Discard the hot water from the pitcher and empty the contents of the glass into the pitcher. Carefully ignite the liquid with a lighter. Slowly swirl the contents back and forth from the sides of the pitcher. Do this 10 times. Carefully pour the fiery contents into a preheated old-fashioned glass. Cover with the bottom of the pitcher to extinguish the flames. Wash the hot pitcher in water immediately. Garnish with a lemon twist.

Old-fashioned

Fragola Fizz

1 strawberry, plus an extra slice
    to garnish
20 ml (⅔ fl oz) fresh lemon juice
15 ml (½ fl oz) sugar syrup (see
    page 9)
15 ml (½ fl oz) egg white
20 ml (⅔ fl oz) Aperol
30 ml (1 fl oz) grappa

Muddle the strawberry in the bottom of a shaker then pour in all the other ingredients. Shake once, without ice, to emulsify the egg white, then a second time with as much ice as possible. Fine-strain into a martini glass. Garnish with a slice of strawberry.

Martini

Gingerbread

15 ml (½ fl oz) cloudy apple juice
10 ml (⅓ fl oz) fresh lemon juice
15 ml (½ fl oz) Monin gingerbread syrup
15 ml (½ fl oz) Appleton Estate V/X rum
30 ml (1 fl oz) vodka
ground cinnamon and caster (superfine) sugar
   to garnish

Put all the ingredients in a cocktail shaker, fill
with ice and shake. Fine-strain into a chilled
martini glass. Mix together some ground
cinnamon and caster sugar and use to dust
the finished cocktail.

Martini

The Oil Change – Motor City

30 ml (1 fl oz) whiskey or vodka
60 ml (2 fl oz/¼ cup) sambuca

Add the whiskey or vodka and the sambuca to
a shaker of ice and strain into a shot glass.

Shot

Gold Leaf

30 ml (1 fl oz) Hennessy VSOP cognac
15 ml (½ fl oz) Joseph Cartron cherry brandy
15 ml (½ fl oz) Toro Albalá Pedro
    Ximenez sherry
10 ml (⅓ fl oz) fresh lemon juice
dash of cocktail bitters
freshly grated nutmeg to dust

⌐

In a Boston shaker, combine all the ingredients over ice. Strain into an old-fashioned glass and dust with nutmeg.

Old-fashioned

The Sagacious Zest

JOE'S SIGNATURE

45 ml (1½ fl oz) orange and sage–infused
    gin (see method)
15 ml (½ fl oz) Cointreau
30 ml (1 fl oz) fresh lemon juice
1 egg white
sage leaf to garnish

⌐

To make the orange and sage–infused gin, soak 1 peeled and segmented orange and 10 sage leaves in a 750 ml (25½ fl oz) bottle of gin. Leave overnight. Remove fruit and leaves.

To make the cocktail, shake all the ingredients thoroughly, without ice first to break down the egg white. When the mixture has a fluffy texture, add ice and shake again. When the shaker feels cold in your hand, it's ready to be poured. Double-strain into a martini glass and garnish with a sage leaf.

Martini

Cuban Cooler

30 ml (1 fl oz) Havana Club 3-year-old rum
30 ml (1 fl oz) Domaine de Canton ginger
   liqueur
15 ml (½ fl oz) fresh lime juice
15 ml (½ fl oz) apple juice
ginger beer
mint sprig to garnish

Build all the ingredients, except the
ginger beer, in a Boston shaker. Fill with
ice, shake and dump into a highball
glass. Top with ginger beer and garnish
with a mint sprig.

Highball

Gin Mule

45 ml (1½ fl oz) Tanqueray gin
15 ml (½ fl oz) El Jimador tequila
½ lime, cut into segments
4–5 mint leaves
ginger beer

Pour the gin and tequila into a highball glass
and lightly muddle with the lime segments. Tear
the mint leaves and place in the glass. Fill with
ice and top with ginger beer. Stir before serving.

Highball

Melbourne Spring Punch

30 ml (1 fl oz) Cariel vanilla vodka
20 ml (⅔ fl oz) fresh lemon juice
10 ml (⅓ fl oz) vanilla gomme syrup
60 ml (2 fl oz/¼ cup) sparkling wine
10 ml (⅓ fl oz) crème de cassis
lemon twist to garnish

Pour the vodka, lemon juice and vanilla gomme into a highball glass. Fill the glass with ice and top with sparkling wine. Float the cassis on top and garnish with a twist of lemon.

Highball

George's Bush

50 ml (1⅔ fl oz) Tanqueray gin
30 ml (1 fl oz) apple juice
20 ml (⅔ fl oz) thyme and pineapple syrup (see method)
20 ml (⅔ fl oz) fresh lemon juice
7–8 mint leaves
Champagne
mint sprig to garnish

To make the thyme and pineapple syrup place 500 ml
(17 fl oz/2 cups) fresh pineapple juice, 250 g (9 oz) caster
(superfine) sugar and 250 ml (8½ fl oz/1 cup) water in a small
saucepan over low heat. Add a small bunch of thyme and stir
gently until the sugar dissolves. Set aside to cool, then strain the
liquid into a bowl covered with muslin (cheesecloth). Put the syrup
in an airtight container and leave it overnight.

To make the cocktail add all the ingredients, except the
Champagne, to a shaker. Shake with ice and strain into an old-
fashioned glass. Crown with crushed ice, top with Champagne
and garnish with the sprig of mint.

Old-fashioned

Black Sambuca Slurp

60 ml (2 fl oz/¼ cup) black sambuca
30 ml (1 fl oz) triple sec or Cointreau
splash of fresh lime juice
splash of sour cherry juice
3 sour cherries to garnish

Half-fill a blender with ice and add all
the ingredients. Blend until it looks like
a slurpee and pour into a highball glass.
Garnish with the sour cherries.

Highball

The Point Lemonade

2 lemons
3 tablespoons caster (superfine) sugar
30 ml (1 fl oz) vodka
30 ml (1 fl oz) mandarin vodka
2 mint sprigs
5 ml (¼ fl oz) orange blossom water
lemon slice and mint sprig to garnish

Cut the lemons into eighths. Muddle with the sugar and leave to macerate for 1 hour. Strain off the liquid and store in the refrigerator. Place the lemon mix, vodkas, mint sprigs and 1 large scoop of ice into a shaker. Shake gently for 10 seconds then pour into a highball glass. Do not strain or remove the ice. Float the orange blossom water on the top and garnish with a lemon slice and a sprig of mint.

Highball

SUGAR

From Italy to Melbourne, with Love ...

45 ml (1½ fl oz) Ketel One vodka
2 dashes of Fee Brothers Peach Bitters
5 ml (¼ fl oz) Monin apple pie syrup
San Pellegrino Pompelmo
2 pink lady apple slices

Add the vodka, bitters and apple pie syrup to a shaker with ice and shake.
Pour into a highball glass and top with San Pellegrino Pompelmo and
garnish with the slices of pink lady apple.

Highball

POST CARD

TO:
Melbourne
with love

ITALY

Waterbar Espressotini

30 ml (1 fl oz) espresso coffee
30 ml (1 fl oz) Belvedere vodka
10 ml (⅓ fl oz) Patrón XO Cafe
10 ml (⅓ fl oz) sugar syrup (see page 9)

Shake all the ingredients with ice and
strain into a martini glass.

Martini

The Phoebe Snow

1 dash of absinthe
30 ml (1 fl oz) brandy

Shake the absinthe and brandy with ice and strain into a chilled martini glass.

Martini

Monsoon

30 ml (1 fl oz) 42 Below honey
   vodka
15 ml (½ fl oz) Joseph Cartron
   Cocody liqueur
15 ml (½ fl oz) lychee liqueur
15 ml (½ fl oz) fresh lemon juice
15 ml (½ fl oz) fresh lime juice
lime slice to garnish

Shake all the ingredients with
ice and strain into a highball
glass. Garnish with a lime slice
on the rim of the glass.

Highball

Pear & Lychee Collins

45 ml (1½ fl oz) Grey Goose La Poire vodka
20 ml (⅔ fl oz) fresh lemon juice
15 ml (½ fl oz) lychee liqueur
15 ml (½ fl oz) sugar syrup (see page 9)
4 lychees, plus 3 extra to garnish
soda water (club soda)

Shake all the ingredients, except the garnish and
the soda water, with ice and strain into a highball
glass. Top with soda water and garnish with
three lychees on a skewer.

Highball

The Red Express

15 ml (½ fl oz) fresh lemon juice
15 ml (½ fl oz) fresh pineapple juice
15 ml (½ fl oz) grenadine
10 ml (⅓ fl oz) sugar syrup (see page 9)
25 ml (¾ fl oz) aged grappa
2 dashes of orange blossom water
Prosecco

Place all the ingredients, except
the Prosecco, into a cocktail
shaker with as much ice as
possible. Shake and strain into
a martini glass and top up
with Prosecco.

Martini

Maple Fizz

maple foam (see method)
45 ml (1½ fl oz) Sazerac rye whiskey
15 ml (½ fl oz) Benedictine
4 dashes each of Fee Brothers Aztec
    Chocolate and Black Walnut Bitters

To make the maple foam, put
90 ml (3 fl oz) maple syrup, 60 ml
(2 fl oz/¼ cup) egg white, 60 ml
(2 fl oz/¼ cup) fresh lemon juice and
30 ml (1 fl oz) water in a whipped
cream charger and shake. Charge once
and then shake again. Chill for an hour.

To make the cocktail, put a little maple
foam into an old-fashioned glass then stir
in the whiskey and Benedictine with ice
and strain into another glass with a julep
strainer. Top with more foam then add
the bitters and swirl with a straw until it
resembles a flat white coffee on top.

Old-fashioned

Windy G&T

3 strawberries
45 ml (1½ fl oz) The West Winds Sabre gin
two 5 cm (2 in) ice cubes with edible
    flowers inside (see method)
3 star anise
Fever-Tree tonic water

To make the edible flower ice cubes, fill
an ice cube tray quarter full with water.
Add flowers face down and freeze. Add
water to top up trays to half full and
freeze again. Fill water to the top of the
tray and freeze again. Ensure you only
use edible flowers and none that have
been sprayed with chemicals.

To make the cocktail, slice the
strawberries and lightly muddle them
inside a collins glass. Pour the gin into
the glass and stir quickly. Drop the ice
cubes and star anise into the glass and
top with tonic until three-quarters full or
to the top of the ice cubes.

Collins

The Luxe
Label Girl

The luxe label girl holds a soft spot for luxury garments; those fashion pieces tailored to her high-end taste buds. She counts on glamorous trends, fashion firsts and boutique finds for her aforementioned loves and when it comes to grooming, it's all about tweaking this with a vive-la-difference spirit.

Her wardrobe is curated according to fashion labels and their sartorial status, she thrives on fashion's seasonal must-haves and owns plenty of outfits only an elite few can call their own. She's an exhibitionist who makes luxury items a daily necessity – fancy price tags aside. She's a modern woman who only allows quality to find a place in her prized wardrobe. She is nostalgic for the future and plots her tipples in much the same fashion. Glamour rates highly in her drinking game – she's all about cocktails that exude confidence, will only drink at the best cocktail bars around the globe and clings to those glasses charmingly dressed with top-shelf spirits that want to look their best at all times.

The Newton

45 ml (1½ fl oz) Laird's Applejack
15 ml (½ fl oz) Aperol
30 ml (1 fl oz) fresh lemon juice
30 ml (1 fl oz) apple balsamic vinegar
10 ml (⅓ fl oz) honey water (half water,
 half honey)
10 ml (⅓ fl oz) grenadine
dash of egg white
paper cut-out apple shape or plastic
 apple stencil to garnish

Shake all the ingredients, add ice
and shake again. Strain into a claret
wine glass and top with a paper
cut-out apple shape or plastic
apple stencil.

Claret

El Matador

30 ml (1 fl oz) tequila
30 ml (1 fl oz) sloe gin
30 ml (1 fl oz) fresh lime juice
2 teaspoons apricot preserve
1 kaffir lime (makrut) leaf to garnish

Shake all the ingredients with ice and
double-strain into a martini glass.
Garnish with a kaffir lime leaf.

Martini

Maldon Gold

15 ml (½ fl oz) Plymouth gin
15 ml (½ fl oz) The Simple Syrup Company
  burnt orange and vanilla bean syrup
15 ml (½ fl oz) Campari
15 ml (½ fl oz) Mandarine Napoléon
15 ml (½ fl oz) fresh lemon juice
soda water (club soda)
lemon and orange twists to garnish

Build the ingredients over crushed ice in
a highball glass, top with soda water and
swizzle. Garnish with lemon and orange
twists. Serve with two paper straws.

Highball

Polish Breeze

45 ml (1½ fl oz) Belvedere vodka
cranberry juice
fresh grapefruit juice
lemon slice to garnish

Pour the vodka into a highball glass
over ice cubes. Top with half cranberry
juice and half grapefruit juice. Garnish
with a slice of lemon.

Highball

Shanghai Sling

45 ml (1½ fl oz) Belvedere vodka
15 ml (½ fl oz) lychee liqueur
10 ml (⅓ fl oz) fresh lemon juice
dash of sugar syrup (see page 9)
pineapple juice
lemon slice to garnish

Build the ingredients in a highball glass
over ice and top with pineapple juice.
Garnish with a slice of lemon.

Highball

Pink Grapefruit Tonic

45 ml (1½ fl oz) Belvedere Pink Grapefruit vodka
tonic water
small pink grapefruit slice to garnish

Build the ingredients in a highball glass
over ice. Garnish with a slice of pink grapefruit.

Highball

Soccer Mum

45 ml (1½ fl oz) Hendrick's gin
1 scoop lemon sorbet
2 dashes of cranberry bitters
45 ml (1½ fl oz) apple juice
10 ml (⅓ fl oz) fresh lemon juice
spray of rosewater mist
3 dried rosebuds to garnish

Shake all the ingredients vigorously with ice and fine-strain into a stemless wine glass. Garnish with the dried rosebuds.

Stemless wine

New York Sour

45 ml (1½ fl oz) rye whisky
30 ml (1 fl oz) fresh lemon juice
15 g (½ oz) sugar
15 ml (½ fl oz) Shiraz

Shake all the ingredients, except the Shiraz,
without ice. Double-strain into an old-fashioned
glass with ice in the bottom. Float the Shiraz
on top.

Old-fashioned

The Real Housewives of Tequila Sunrise

45 ml (1½ fl oz) Jose Cuervo Tradicional tequila
45 ml (1½ fl oz) jasmine tea
15 ml (½ fl oz) pomegranate syrup, plus
   1 teaspoon to finish
15 ml (½ fl oz) fresh pineapple juice
10 ml (⅓ fl oz) caramel liqueur
15 ml (½ fl oz) fresh lemon juice
1 dash of Fee Brothers Orange Bitters
1 maraschino cherry to garnish
1 orange wedge to garnish

Shake all the ingredients with ice. Strain into
an ice-filled wine glass. Float the additional
pomegranate syrup on top. Garnish with a
cherry and wedge of orange.

Wine

Touche Par L' Amour

30 ml (1 fl oz) Martin Miller's gin
30 ml (1 fl oz) Champagne
20 ml (⅔ fl oz) rosewater
15 ml (½ fl oz) fresh lemon juice
15 ml (½ fl oz) sugar syrup (see page 9)
2 dashes of cherry bitters
3 muddled strawberries
2 tablespoons whipped cream,
  sweetened with a little sugar
1 maraschino cherry and 1 mint sprig
  to garnish

Combine the ingredients, except the
cream, in an old-fashioned glass with
crushed ice. Top with more crushed
ice and the sweetened whipped
cream. Garnish with a maraschino
cherry and a mint sprig.

Old-fashioned

Rum & Aperol Sour

45 ml (1½ fl oz) Havana Club 3-year-old rum
15 ml (½ fl oz) Aperol
30 ml (1 fl oz) fresh lemon juice
15 ml (½ fl oz) sugar syrup (see page 9)
1 egg white

Dry-shake all the ingredients. Add ice and shake vigorously. Double-strain into a chilled coupette glass.

Coupette

Flapjacket #1

150 ml (5 fl oz) Russian caravan tea
75 ml (2½ fl oz) sweet vermouth
2 teaspoons orgeat syrup
dash of orange bitters
spray of Laphroaig single malt whisky
  to finish

Fill an ice-cube tray with Russian
caravan tea and freeze. Fill an
old-fashioned glass with the
tea-infused ice cubes. Build the
remaining ingredients and finish
with a spray of Laphroaig single
malt whisky.

Old-fashioned

Pineapple Mary

45 ml (1½ fl oz) Belvedere Bloody
  Mary vodka
15 ml (½ fl oz) fresh lemon juice
dash of Tabasco sauce
fresh pineapple juice
lemon slice and cracked black pepper
  to garnish

Build and stir the vodka, lemon juice
and Tabasco sauce in a highball glass
over ice. Top with pineapple juice and
garnish with a slice of lemon and some
cracked black pepper.

Highball

In Violet

caster (superfine) sugar to rim glass
30 ml (1 fl oz) Belvedere Citrus vodka
15 ml (½ fl oz) violet liqueur
15 ml (½ fl oz) St Germain elderflower liqueur
handful of muddled blueberries
Champagne
fresh blueberries and a lemon twist to garnish

Dip the rim of a Champagne flute in
the caster sugar. Add the vodka, violet
liqueur and St Germain and stir to
combine. Add the muddled blueberries
and top with Champagne. Garnish with
blueberries and a twist of lemon.

Champagne flute

La Dolce Vita

30 ml (1 fl oz) Campari
30 ml (1 fl oz) Averna
30 ml (1 fl oz) Noilly Prat vermouth
cream soda

Build the ingredients in a wine glass
over ice cubes. Top up with cream soda.

Wine

Florabotanica

45 ml (1½ fl oz) The West Winds Sabre gin
15 ml (½ fl oz) yuzu juice
15 ml (½ fl oz) rose syrup
15 ml (½ fl oz) apple liqueur
2 thyme sprigs
4 dashes of dandelion and burdock bitters
dehydrated orange slice and blue dragon
    flower to garnish

Shake all the ingredients with ice and strain into
an old-fashioned glass. Garnish with the orange
slice and blue dragon flower.

Old-fashioned

Spicy Mango

45 ml (1 ½ fl oz) Belvedere Bloody Mary vodka
45 ml (1 ½ fl oz) mango purée
15 ml (½ fl oz) fresh lemon juice
cracked black pepper to garnish

Shake all the ingredients with ice and strain
into a martini glass. Garnish with some cracked
black pepper.

Martini

The Venus Fly Trap

25 ml (¾ fl oz) apple brandy
25 ml (¾ fl oz) St Germain elderflower liqueur
25 ml (¾ fl oz) Lillet Blanc vermouth
25 ml (¾ fl oz) pineapple juice
lemon twist to garnish

Shake all the ingredients with ice and
fine-strain into a coupette glass. Garnish
with a twist of lemon.

Coupette

After Dinner Mint

30 ml (1 fl oz) Cariel vanilla vodka
25 ml (¾ fl oz) Mozart chocolate liqueur
12.5 ml (⅓ fl oz) crème de menthe
20 ml (⅔ fl oz) vanilla syrup
20 ml (⅔ fl oz) milk
20 ml (⅔ fl oz) cream
chocolate swirls and milk arrowroot biscuits
  (cookies) to garnish

Shake all the ingredients with ice and fine-strain
into a chilled martini glass. Garnish with the
chocolate swirls and milk arrowroot biscuit, either
crumbled on top or placed on the side.

Martini

Lil' Tom Thumb

45 ml (1½ fl oz) rye whisky
20 ml (⅔ fl oz) fresh lemon juice
10 ml (⅓ fl oz) apricot brandy
1 teaspoon plum jam
dash of vanilla syrup
dash of Fee Brothers Whiskey
   Barrel-Aged Bitters
dehydrated lemon slice and a
   maraschino cherry to garnish

Shake all the ingredients with ice
and strain into a jam jar. Garnish
with a dehydrated slice of lemon
and a maraschino cherry.

Jam jar

Macedon Gang Punch

45 ml (1½ fl oz) Cruzan rum
30 ml (1 fl oz) fresh lemon juice
20 ml (⅔ fl oz) Crawley's Bartender agave syrup
15 ml (½ fl oz) egg white
5 ml (¼ fl oz) port
blast of Booker's Fire Bitters (see method)

For the Booker's Fire Bitters, fill an olive oil
pump spray with Booker's bourbon. Then
compress/pump. (This will now be a veritable
flamethrower!) Add 25 ml (¾ fl oz) angostura
bitters on top. (Makes 1 bottle, enough for
30–40 cocktails.)

Shake all the ingredients with ice, except the
Booker's Fire Bitters. Pour into a chilled coupette
glass and carefully spray a blast of Booker's Fire
Bitters over the drink through a flame.

Coupette

Aomomo Sidecar

4 peeled baby green peaches
20 ml (⅔ fl oz) aomomo (Japanese peach) juice
40 ml (1⅓ fl oz) Hennessy VSOP cognac
10 ml (⅓ fl oz) crème de peche
10 ml (⅓ fl oz) Cointreau
20 ml (⅔ fl oz) fresh lemon juice

Muddle 3 of the peaches with the juice. Add all the
other ingredients and shake with ice. Double-strain
into a martini glass. Garnish with the remaining
peach, cut into decorative slices.

Martini

Tall Poppy

2 fresh cherries
25 ml (¾ fl oz) Absolut Citron vodka
25 ml (¾ fl oz) Aperol
25 ml (¾ fl oz) fresh lemon juice
12.5 ml (⅓ fl oz) Monin vanilla syrup
Prosecco or sparkling wine
lemon twist to garnish

Muddle the cherries in a shaker. Add the other
ingredients, except the Prosecco, and shake
with ice. Fine-strain into a Champagne flute.
Top with the Prosecco or sparkling wine and
garnish with a lemon twist.

Champagne

First Spring

60 ml (2 fl oz/¼ cup) gin
30 ml (1 fl oz) fresh lime juice
25 ml (¾ fl oz) grenadine
1 teaspoon sugar syrup (see page 9)
4 mint leaves and 1 cm (½ in) slice of
   cucumber to garnish

Muddle and shake all the ingredients with ice
and fine-strain into a martini glass. Garnish with
mint leaves and a slice of cucumber.

Martini

Breakfast Negroni

30 ml (1 fl oz) Belvedere Bloody Mary vodka
20 ml (⅔ fl oz) Campari
20 ml (⅔ fl oz) rosso vermouth
20 ml (⅔ fl oz) tomato juice
orange slice and cracked black pepper to garnish

Stir the ingredients over ice in an old-fashioned glass. Garnish with a slice of orange and some cracked black pepper.

Old-fashioned

The Bohemian Girl

She's one part protest hippie and two measures gypsy wannabe – yes, the bohemian girl is distilled proof that the spirit of the '60s and '70s is relevant. She's hippie free love meets prairie cool, and is as inspired by psychedelic prints and geometric folk patterns as she is by embroidery and the need for it to be – well – almost everywhere. She'll give peace a chance and, if time machines worked, she'd be right back on the 1960s Parisian streets all in the name of the sexual revolution. The bohemian femme steps back in time and hunts the archives making sure there's a '70s throwback in her modern moves. She's not fussed by time's passing; rather she borrows from its decadent history in her effort to keep all that has come before relevant and new. She channels Jane Birkin and Jerry Hall – during her 1970s Yves Saint Laurent modelling spell – and adds the finer quirks of her fashion styling thanks to music icons like Joan Baez and Marianne Faithfull.

When it comes to her drinks, she'd crochet a cosy for her drinking glass if she could and, when it comes to flavour, the bohemian hunts down those cocktails brimming with a vagabond spirit always ready for the next adventure with every sip.

Pink Aperol Spritz

30 ml (1 fl oz) Belvedere Pink Grapefruit vodka
30 ml (1 fl oz) Aperol
15 ml (½ fl oz) fresh pink grapefruit juice
15 ml (½ fl oz) sugar syrup (see page 9)
soda water (club soda)
orange slice to garnish

Build in a wine glass and top up with soda water.
Garnish with an orange slice.

Wine

Lemon Drop Martini

45 ml (1 ½ fl oz) Belvedere Citrus vodka
15 ml (½ fl oz) Limoncello
15 ml (½ fl oz) fresh lemon juice
15 ml (½ fl oz) sugar syrup (see page 9)
lemon twist to garnish

Shake all the ingredients with ice and strain
into a martini glass. Garnish with a lemon twist.

Martini

Peaches Geldof

30 ml (1 fl oz) Ketel One vodka
30 ml (1 fl oz) elderflower syrup
30 ml (1 fl oz) fresh lemon juice
30 ml (1 fl oz) sugar syrup (see page 9)
Prosecco
mint sprig, a pink flower petal and a lemon wedge
  to garnish

Shake the ingredients, except the Prosecco and
garnishes, with ice. Strain into a wine glass, fill with
ice and top with the Prosecco. Garnish with a sprig
of mint, a pink flower petal and a lemon wedge.

Wine

Janis Joplin

50 ml (1⅔ fl oz) chamomile tea–infused Jack Daniel's
  (see method)
15 ml (½ fl oz) white crème de cacao
20 ml (⅔ fl oz) Cointreau
30 ml (1 fl oz) fresh lemon juice
10 ml (⅓ fl oz) pineapple syrup
1 rosebud to garnish

To make the chamomile tea-infused Jack
Daniel's, place 25 g (1 oz/1 cup) chamomile
tea leaves in a 700 ml (23½ fl oz) bottle of Jack
Daniel's and leave to sit for 30 minutes.

To make the cocktail, shake all the ingredients
with ice and fine-strain into a coupette glass.
Garnish with a rosebud.

Coupette

Full Moon

60 ml (2 fl oz/¼ cup) gin
25 ml (¾ fl oz) fresh lemon juice
25 ml (¾ fl oz) sugar syrup (see page 9)
3 blackberries, plus 1 extra to garnish
1 egg white

Dry-shake all the ingredients, then
shake with ice and strain into a martini
glass. Garnish with a blackberry.

Martini

Kamikaze

30 ml (1 fl oz) vodka
30 ml (1 fl oz) triple sec
30 ml (1 fl oz) fresh lime juice
lime slice to garnish

Shake all the ingredients in a mixer
with ice. Strain into a martini glass
and garnish with a lime slice.

Martini

Citrus Solstice

30 ml (1 fl oz) homemade lemonade
15 ml (½ fl oz) crème de gingembre
15 ml (½ fl oz) honey liqueur
30 ml (1 fl oz) Four Roses Irish whiskey
5 ml (¼ fl oz) Oban whiskey
crystallised ginger to garnish

Stir and strain all the ingredients,
except the Oban whiskey and ginger,
into an ice-filled old-fashioned glass.
Float the Oban whiskey on top and
garnish with the crystallised ginger.

Old-fashioned

Citrus Apple Martini

45 ml (1½ fl oz) Belvedere Citrus vodka
15 ml (½ fl oz) green apple liqueur
10 ml (⅓ fl oz) fresh lime juice
20 ml (⅔ fl oz) cloudy apple juice
slice of apple to garnish

Shake all the ingredients with ice and strain into
a martini glass. Garnish with a slice of apple.

Martini

Clover Leaf

35 ml (1¼ fl oz) gin
5 ml (¼ fl oz) sweet vermouth
5 ml (¼ fl oz) dry vermouth
25 ml (¾ fl oz) raspberry syrup
25 ml (¾ fl oz) fresh lemon juice
15 ml (½ fl oz) egg white
mint leaf to garnish

Dry-shake all the ingredients, then shake with ice and strain into a coupette or martini glass. Garnish with a mint leaf.

Coupette or martini

Rum Shrub

12 raspberries
1 strawberry
45 ml (1½ fl oz) Jamaican rum
15 ml (½ fl oz) crème de framboise
2 dashes of angostura bitters
10 ml (⅓ fl oz) sugar syrup (see page 9)

Muddle the fruit in a shaker. Add all the other ingredients, shake and single-strain into a coupette glass.

Coupette

Nuggety Gully

45 ml (1½ fl oz) paperbark-infused
    Cruzan rum (see method)
8–10 mint leaves
6 chunks of lime
15 ml (½ fl oz) sugar syrup (see page 9)
Bundaberg ginger beer
dash of angostura bitters
mint sprigs to garnish

To make the paperbark-infused rum you need an 8 cm (3¼ in) piece of fresh paperbark and 1 bottle (700 ml/23½ fl oz) Cruzan rum. Place the roll of paperbark into the rum. Leave overnight, then strain and bottle.

To make the cocktail, build all the ingredients in a highball glass over crushed ice and swizzle. Garnish with the mint sprigs and serve with two paper straws.

Highball

Bund Glam

6 strawberries, plus 1 extra to garnish
60 ml (2 fl oz/¼ cup) vodka
30 ml (1 fl oz) sugar syrup (see page 9)
soda water (club soda)
strawberry to garnish

Muddle the 6 strawberries then add all
the other ingredients, except the soda
water. Pour into a highball glass with
ice. Top with soda water and garnish
with the extra strawberry.

Highball

Little Rosey

15 ml (½ fl oz) Monin rose syrup
30 ml (1 fl oz) Tanqueray gin
15 ml (½ fl oz) Vincent Van Gogh pineapple vodka
15 ml (½ fl oz) Belvedere Citrus vodka
5 ml (¼ fl oz) fresh lemon juice
red edible flower to garnish

Shake all the ingredients with ice and double-strain into a martini glass. Garnish with a red edible flower.

Martini

Talbot Town Tipple

15 ml (½ fl oz) spiced pumpkin and cider liqueur (see method)
15 ml (½ fl oz) Crawley's Bartender orgeat syrup
60 ml (2 fl oz/¼ cup) James Squire Orchard Crush apple cider
45 ml (1½ fl oz) Laird's Applejack
15 ml (½ fl oz) fresh lemon juice
30 ml (1 fl oz) fresh orange juice
3 dashes of Fee Brothers Celery Bitters
pinch of ground cinnamon
lemon twist to garnish

To make the spiced pumpkin and cider liqueur you need 700 ml (23½ fl oz)
apple cider, 1 medium-sized pumpkin (squash) chopped into 10 chunks, 1.1 kg
(2 lb 7 oz) caster (superfine) sugar, 200 ml (7 fl oz) Laird's Applejack, a pinch of
allspice, 2 cloves, 1 teaspoon ground cinnamon and 1 teaspoon freshly grated
nutmeg. On the stovetop pour the cider into a hot saucepan. Add the pumpkin
and cook over a low heat until the pumpkin is softened but still intact. Turn off the
heat, add the spices and allow to cool. Strain and bottle. This makes enough for
30–40 cocktails. Keep refrigerated.

To make the cocktail, build all the ingredients over crushed ice and swizzle.
Garnish with a lemon twist and serve in a highball glass with two paper straws.

Highball

Coriander Smack

3 coriander (cilantro) stems, with leaves and root
5 ml (¼ fl oz) yuzu juice
45 ml (1½ fl oz) mango vodka
15 ml (½ fl oz) De Kuyper Sour Apple Pucker
15 ml (½ fl oz) peach schnapps
30 ml (1 fl oz) pineapple purée
coriander (cilantro) leaf to garnish

Muddle the coriander root. Add the other
ingredients, shake with ice and double-
strain into a martini glass. Garnish with
a coriander leaf.

Martini

Godmother

45 ml (1½ fl oz) Belvedere vodka
15 ml (½ fl oz) amaretto
maraschino cherry to garnish

Build over ice in an old-fashioned glass and
stir. Garnish with a maraschino cherry.

Old-fashioned

Vanilla Sling

30 ml (1 fl oz) Belvedere vodka
15 ml (½ fl oz) vanilla liqueur
dash of bitters
pineapple juice
orange slice to garnish

Build the cocktail in a highball glass
over ice. Garnish with an orange slice.

Highball

Pink Ginger Mule

45 ml (1½ fl oz) Belvedere Pink Grapefruit
  vodka
15 ml (½ fl oz) Domaine de Canton ginger
  liqueur
ginger beer
lime wedge to garnish

Build the cocktail in a highball glass
over ice and top with ginger beer.
Garnish with a lime wedge.

Highball

Fantastic Fizz

45 ml (1½ fl oz) Tanqueray gin
15 ml (½ fl oz) Aperol
5 ml (¼ fl oz) absinthe
20 ml (⅔ fl oz) passionfruit liqueur
25 ml (¾ fl oz) fresh lemon juice
10 ml (⅓ fl oz) falernum
10 ml (⅓ fl oz) sugar syrup (see page 9)
dash of egg white
Fanta
orange twist and star anise to garnish

Dry-shake then shake all the
ingredients, except the Fanta, with
ice cubes. Pour into a highball glass
and top with Fanta. Garnish with the
orange twist and star anise.

Highball

Breakfast Apple Fizz

45 ml (1½ fl oz) Belvedere Bloody Mary vodka
15 ml (½ fl oz) apple liqueur
15 ml (½ fl oz) cloudy apple juice
soda water (club soda)
slice of cucumber to garnish

Build all the ingredients in a highball glass over ice and top up with soda water. Stir and garnish with a slice of cucumber.

Highball

Frisco Sour

50 ml (1⅔ fl oz) Rittenhouse Rye whisky
10 ml (⅓ fl oz) Benedictine
20 ml (⅔ fl oz) fresh lemon juice
10 ml (⅓ fl oz) sugar syrup (see page 9)

⌒

Dry-shake all the ingredients. Add ice and
shake vigorously. Double-strain into a chilled
coupette glass.

Coupette

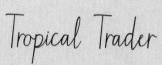

Tropical Trader

50 ml (1⅔ fl oz) Ron Matusalem
   Platino rum
10 ml (⅓ fl oz) lemon myrtle liqueur
20 ml (⅔ fl oz) fresh lime juice
10 ml (⅓ fl oz) pineapple juice
15 ml (½ fl oz) sugar syrup (see page 9)
5 ml (¼ fl oz) yuzu curd

Shake with ice and strain all the ingredients
into an old-fashioned glass with ice cubes.

Old-fashioned

Peanut Butter Jelly Time

muddled peanuts and raspberries to rim glass
60 ml (2 fl oz/¼ cup) peanut rum
10 ml (⅓ fl oz) Clément Créole Shrubb liqueur
10 ml (⅓ fl oz) Joseph Cartron crème de cassis
5 ml (¼ fl oz) Frangelico
10 ml (⅓ fl oz) fresh lemon juice
3 dashes of Fee Brothers Plum Bitters

Rim a claret glass by dipping it into the muddled peanuts
and raspberries. Shake all the ingredients with ice and
fine-strain into the claret glass.

Claret

Disco Biscuits

30 ml (1 fl oz) 42 Below Passionfruit
   vodka
30 ml (1 fl oz) passionfruit purée
10 ml (⅓ fl oz) Wattle Toffee Liqueur
10 ml (⅓ fl oz) apricot brandy
10 ml (⅓ fl oz) fresh lemon juice
5 ml (¼ fl oz) sugar syrup (see page 9)
soda water (club soda)
mint leaf and a cherry to garnish

⌣

Shake all the ingredients with ice
and strain into a wine glass. Fill
with ice. Garnish with a mint leaf
and a cherry.

Wine

Fruit Tingle

30 ml (1 fl oz) blue curaçao
30 ml (1 fl oz) vodka
lemonade
dash of raspberry cordial

⌒

Pour the blue curaçao and vodka
over ice in a highball glass. Top
with lemonade and add a dash of
raspberry cordial.

Highball

Pina Colada

60 ml (2 fl oz/¼ cup) white rum
30 ml (1 fl oz) coconut milk
60 ml (2 fl oz/¼ cup) fresh pineapple juice
20 ml (⅔ fl oz) fresh lime juice
pineapple wedge to garnish

⌒

Blend all the ingredients in a blender
with ice until slush-like. Pour into a
hurricane glass and garnish with
a pineapple wedge.

Hurricane

Sunny Sailor's Fluffy Duck

30 ml (1 fl oz) light rum
30 ml (1 fl oz) advocaat
15 ml (½ fl oz) Cointreau
30 ml (1 fl oz) pouring (single/light) cream
30 ml (1 fl oz) fresh orange juice
30 ml (1 fl oz) lemonade

Mix the rum, advocaat, Cointreau, cream and orange juice
in a shaker with ice. Strain into a large martini glass and top
with the lemonade.

Martini

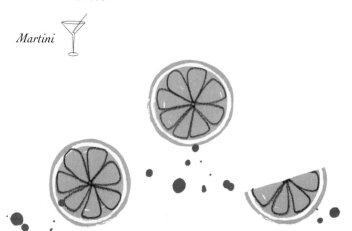

Raspberry Beret

1 dessertspoon raspberry sorbet
45 ml (1½ fl oz) Ketel One vodka
15 ml (½ fl oz) white crème de cacao
15 ml (½ fl oz) fresh lemon juice
10 ml (⅓ fl oz) sugar syrup (see page 9)
dash of Fee Brothers Aztec Chocolate Bitters
mint leaf to garnish

Shake all the ingredients with ice and fine-strain into a martini glass. Garnish with a mint leaf.

Martini

The Hipster Girl

The hipster girl wants to be seen and heard, takes cues from those who break fashion's rules to reinvent as her own, and sides with the couture outlaws all in the name of being hip. The hipster belongs in life's fast lane – she's a blogger's delight and uses Instagram to post photos of herself to create her own brand of cool, saluting her fashion finds along the way. Nothing sticks around long enough to put her in a bad mood, for the hipster girl is onto something new before the hip becomes tragic. She lives life on the fringe (usually somewhere in hip suburbia) and refines her look from thrift-store purchases to labels that are new kids on the block of cool-dom. She is the ultimate consumer of all things popular, and swiftly moves from one season to the next, ready to put her own finishing touches on what she calls fashion.

When it comes to drinking, the hipster makes sure her liquor cabinet is stocked with the spirits that matter, ready to show off her bar skills to friends willing to sit through her mantra of what they ought to be drinking.

Tio's Margarita

salt to garnish
40 ml (1⅓ fl oz) tequila
20 ml (⅔ fl oz) Cointreau
30 ml (1 fl oz) fresh lime juice

Salt the rim of a wine glass. Shake all
the ingredients with ice and serve in
the wine glass.

Wine

Hard Eight

25 ml (¾ fl oz) sage syrup (see method)
sugar and black pepper to garnish
2 blackberries
1 cm (½ in) slice of jalapeño
50 ml (1⅔ fl oz) tequila ocho
15 ml (½ fl oz) crème de mure
25 ml (¾ fl oz) fresh lime juice

To make the sage syrup, gently heat 250 ml
(8½ fl oz/1 cup) water with 220 g (7½ oz/1 cup)
sugar in a small saucepan over low heat. Add
10 g (¼ oz/½ cup) sage leaves and simmer for
15 minutes. Remove from the heat, strain the
leaves from the syrup and discard.

To make the cocktail, rim an old-fashioned
glass with sugar and black pepper. Muddle
the blackberries and jalapeño slice. Add the
remaining ingredients and shake. Fine-strain
into the glass with ice cubes.

Old-fashioned

La Cosa Nostra

50 ml (1⅔ fl oz) bourbon
25 ml (¾ fl oz) Averna
10 ml (⅓ fl oz) amaretto
2 drops of Fee Brothers Aztec Chocolate Bitters
twist of orange to garnish

Stir all the ingredients in a mixing glass with ice. Julep-strain into a chilled martini glass and garnish with a twist of orange.

Martini

Bloody Mary Spritz

45 ml (1½ fl oz) Belvedere Bloody Mary vodka
dash of Tabasco sauce
30 ml (1 fl oz) tomato juice
soda water (club soda)
1 cherry tomato and cracked black pepper to garnish

Build the ingredients in a wine glass with ice
and top with soda water. Garnish with the cherry
tomato and some cracked black pepper.

Wine

Pink Sling

45 ml (1½ fl oz) Belvedere Pink
   Grapefruit vodka
60 ml (2 fl oz/¼ cup) cranberry juice
soda water (club soda)
2 lime wedges to garnish

Build the ingredients with ice in a
highball glass and top with soda water.
Garnish with wedges of lime.

Highball

Toreador

25 ml (¾ fl oz) tequila blanco
25 ml (¾ fl oz) apricot liqueur
25 ml (¾ fl oz) fresh lime juice
1 teaspoon agave nectar
twist of lime to garnish

Shake with ice and double-strain
into a coupette or martini glass.
Garnish with a twist of lime.

Coupette or martini

Nitro Punch

SERVES 6

200 ml (7 fl oz) Ketel One Citroen vodka
60 ml (2 fl oz/¼ cup) St Germain
   elderflower liqueur
100 ml (3½ fl oz) fresh lemon juice
50 ml (1⅔ fl oz) sugar syrup (see page 9)
100 ml (3½ fl oz) tea infusion
   (2:1 Russian caravan and oolong berry)
5 dashes of grapefruit bitters
dehydrated citrus slice to garnish

Build the ingredients over ice cubes in a
punch bowl. Garnish with a dehydrated
citrus slice.

Punch

Belvedere Bloody Mary

45 ml (1½ fl oz) Belvedere Bloody Mary vodka
dash of Tabasco sauce
10 ml (⅓ fl oz) fresh lemon juice
tomato juice
slice of lemon and cracked black pepper to garnish

Build the ingredients with ice in a highball glass and
top with tomato juice. Garnish with a slice of lemon
and some cracked black pepper.

Highball

Smoky Castro

60 ml (2 fl oz/¼ cup) Cohiba cigar–infused
   Glenmorangie Scotch whisky (see method)
1 teaspoon good-quality unsweetened
   cocoa powder
1 hot ristretto coffee
1 teaspoon brown sugar
chocolate shavings to garnish

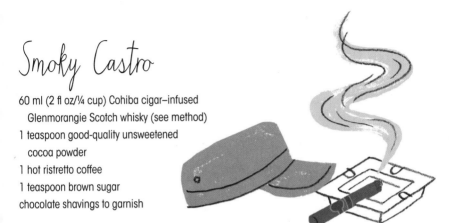

To infuse the whisky, place a Cohiba cigar
in a bottle of Glenmorangie and leave in a
dry, cool place for 2 weeks. Remove the cigar
before using.

To make the cocktail, add all the ingredients to a
shaker and heat in a saucepan of water over low
heat to 75°C (165°F). Pour into a large brandy
snifter and serve on a wooden chopping board
with some shaved chocolate to garnish.

Brandy snifter

Barrel Full of Monkeys

50 ml (1⅔ fl oz) banana–infused Scotch whisky
  (see method)
30 ml (1 fl oz) fresh lemon juice
15 ml (½ fl oz) white chocolate syrup
15 ml (½ fl oz) egg white
toy plastic monkey barrel and plastic monkey
  to garnish

To infuse the whisky, peel and slice
3 bananas and place in a 1 litre (34 fl oz/4 cup)
capacity jar. Add one 750 ml (25 fl oz) bottle of
Scotch whisky, seal tightly and leave to infuse for
3–4 days. Strain the whisky back into its bottle.

To make the cocktail, shake the ingredients
briefly without ice. Add ice and shake vigorously.
Double-strain into a small old-fashioned glass
placed inside a toy monkey barrel. Garnish with
a plastic monkey.

Old-fashioned

Spiced Fig & Pear Daiquiri

45 ml (1½ fl oz) Bacardi Oro
30 ml (1 fl oz) pear nectar
15 ml (½ fl oz) fresh lime juice
15 ml (½ fl oz) spice syrup (see page 9)
1 teaspoon fig jam
½ fresh fig to garnish

Shake all the ingredients with ice and pour into
a small, chilled pitcher. Garnish with the fig and
serve with a coloured straw.

Small pitcher

Beechworth Gunpowder

45 ml (1½ fl oz) Cruzan rum
30 ml (1 fl oz) fresh lime juice
15 ml (½ fl oz) pineapple and almond syrup
30 ml (1 fl oz) ginger beer
unsweetened pineapple juice
splash of Laphroaig single malt whisky
twists of lemon to garnish

Build all the ingredients in a highball glass over crushed ice and swizzle. Garnish with twists of lemon and serve with two paper straws.

Highball

Pepe's Punchy Pear

50 ml (1⅔ fl oz) Cuervo Tradicional tequila
15 ml (½ fl oz) fresh lemon juice
15 g (½ oz) vanilla sugar
30 ml (1 fl oz) pear purée
30 ml (1 fl oz) apple juice
dash of egg white

Vigorously shake the ingredients, add ice cubes and shake again. Strain over ice cubes in an old-fashioned glass.

Old-fashioned

I Love Ewan McGregor

45 ml (1½ fl oz) Caorunn gin
15 ml (½ fl oz) fresh lemon juice
10 ml (⅓ fl oz) gomme syrup
1 teaspoon violette liqueur
3 dashes of rhubarb bitters
1 teaspoon grenadine to finish

Shake all the ingredients, except the grenadine, with ice and strain into a chilled martini glass. Gently drop the grenadine into the centre of the drink and watch it sink.

Martini

Pink Grapefruit Cosmo

45 ml (1½ fl oz) Belvedere Pink Grapefruit vodka
15 ml (½ fl oz) Cointreau
2 lime wedges
30 ml (1 fl oz) fresh pink grapefruit juice
lime slice to garnish

Shake the ingredients with ice and strain into
a martini glass. Garnish with a slice of lime.

Martini

Frosty Passionfruit

45 ml (1½ fl oz) Belvedere Citrus vodka
15 ml (½ fl oz) peach liqueur
15 ml (½ fl oz) fresh lemon juice
10 ml (⅓ fl oz) sugar syrup (see page 9)
15 ml (½ fl oz) passionfruit pulp

Shake all the ingredients, except the passionfruit
pulp, with ice and strain into a martini glass. Top
with the passionfruit pulp.

Martini

Cellared Milk Rum Punch

SERVES 6–8

zest of 3 lemons
345 g (12 oz/1½ cups) caster (superfine) sugar
135 ml (4½ fl oz) fresh lemon juice
1.5 litres (51 fl oz/ 6 cups) white or dark rum
750 ml (25½ fl oz/3 cups) full-cream (whole) milk
½ nutmeg, freshly grated

In a large bowl combine the lemon zest and sugar and leave for 1 hour. Muddle and add the lemon juice. Stir until the sugar dissolves, then add the rum.

Heat the milk on the stovetop until scalding hot. Add the hot milk to the lemon and rum mixture and stir as it curdles. Stir in the freshly grated nutmeg and let the mixture sit for 1 hour.

Strain the liquid through muslin (cheesecloth) into sterilised bottles. Pop the punch into the freezer until it becomes clear. Serve in a punch bowl.

Punch

Gobbler Cobbler

40 ml (1⅓ fl oz) Wild Turkey American
   honey whiskey
20 ml (⅔ fl oz) Manzanilla dry sherry
lemon wedge to garnish
orange wedge to garnish
dash of angostura bitters to garnish
mint sprig to garnish

Build the ingredients with ice in a
wine glass. Garnish with a lemon
and orange wedge, a dash of bitters
and a sprig of mint.

Wine

Citrus Fizz

45 ml (1½ fl oz) Belvedere Citrus vodka
15 ml (½ fl oz) Cointreau
30 ml (1 fl oz) fresh orange juice
15 ml (½ fl oz) fresh lemon juice
dash of bitters
orange slice to garnish

Build ingredients with ice in a highball
glass. Garnish with a slice of orange.

Highball

El Oso Goloso

50 ml (1⅔ fl oz) tequila
10 ml (⅓ fl oz) maraschino liqueur
30 ml (1 fl oz) pineapple juice
20 ml (⅔ fl oz) fresh lime juice
10 ml (⅓ fl oz) agave syrup
dash of bitters
mint leaves to garnish
pineapple slice to garnish

Shake all the ingredients, except the bitters and garnishes, with ice. Pour into a sling glass with ice. Add a dash of bitters and garnish with mint leaves and a slice of pineapple.

Sling

Old Cuban

40 ml (1⅓ fl oz) white rum
30 ml (1 fl oz) fresh lime juice
15 g (½ oz) sugar
dash of angostura bitters
30 ml (1 fl oz) Champagne
6 mint leaves to garnish

Shake all the ingredients, except the Champagne, with ice. Add the Champagne to the shaker, then double-strain into a coupette or martini glass. Garnish with mint leaves.

Coupette or martini

Pink Grapefruit & White Chocolate Sling

45 ml (1½ fl oz) Belvedere Pink Grapefruit vodka
15 ml (½ fl oz) white crème de cacao
15 ml (½ fl oz) fresh lime juice
soda water (club soda)
slice of small pink grapefruit to garnish

Build the ingredients with ice in a highball glass.
Garnish with a slice of pink grapefruit.

Highball

The Haute
Couture Girl

The world of haute couture is reserved for fashion's most labour-intensive dresses and pieces, considered art forms in their own right. Extravagance dominates and lovers of all things made-to-order and hand-sewn adore couture for its pantomime nature. This is theatre meets fairytale dreaming, elegance veering on the edge of dangerous, and fancy gowns that take hundreds of hours to sew – only to gain a few moments in the limelight on international runways each year. The couture woman adores those fashion houses that deliver exuberant collections each year, such as Chanel, Dior and Valentino. It's where she can dream a little and live a lot – through the beauty of fabric and the genius of designers; and hold hands with the avant garde and be beguiled by fashion's intricate ways.

In her finest cocktail hour the couture woman will fuss over minute details, follow the classic drinks defined by elegance and obsess over all things French. She is inspired by glamour, thrives on creative impulse and chooses her spirits in much the same fashion. Lured by couture's often obscure and always decadent modus operandi, she's just as impressed when her drinks take the road less travelled if it means she's bound to have more fun.

Versailles Experience

SERVES 4

200 ml (7 fl oz) Tanqueray gin
100 ml (3½ fl oz) fresh lemon juice
40 ml (1⅓ fl oz) jasmine syrup
60 ml (2 fl oz/¼ cup) Joseph Cartron Poire William
60 ml (2 fl oz/¼ cup) pear purée
16 mint leaves, plus extra to garnish
60 ml (2 fl oz/¼ cup) La Fée absinthe
180 ml (6 fl oz) apple juice

Shake all the ingredients, except the absinthe and half the apple juice. Double-strain into martini glasses and garnish with the extra mint leaves. Add the absinthe, remaining apple juice and ice cubes to an absinthe fountain and serve.

Martini glasses and absinthe fountain

The 42Nd Street

40 ml (1⅓ fl oz) bourbon
10 ml (⅓ fl oz) Grand Marnier
10 ml (⅓ fl oz) Cointreau
10 ml (⅓ fl oz) dry vermouth
lemon twist and a maraschino cherry to garnish

Stir all the ingredients with ice and strain into
a martini glass. Garnish with a lemon twist
and a maraschino cherry.

Martini

French 75

30 ml (1 fl oz) gin or cognac
15 ml (½ fl oz) fresh lemon juice
15 ml (½ fl oz) sugar syrup (see page 9)
60 ml (2 fl oz/¼ cup) Champagne
lemon twist to garnish

Fill a cocktail shaker with ice and add
the gin or cognac, lemon juice and
syrup. Shake then strain into a chilled
Champagne flute. Top with Champagne
and garnish with a lemon twist.

Champagne

Citrus Sling

45 ml (1½ fl oz) Belvedere Citrus vodka
15 ml (½ fl oz) vanilla liqueur
dash of bitters
15 ml (½ fl oz) fresh lemon juice
pineapple juice
orange slice to garnish

Build all the ingredients in a highball
glass with ice. Garnish with an
orange slice.

Highball

The Diversity Cocktail

45 ml (1½ fl oz) Bowmore 12-year-old
   single malt whisky
15 ml (½ fl oz) Lena banana liqueur
15 ml (½ fl oz) yellow Chartreuse
dash of Fee Brothers Whiskey Barrel-Aged
   Bitters
lemon twist to garnish

Stir all the ingredients with ice and
strain into a coupette glass. Garnish
with a lemon twist.

Coupette

Q-Tip's Curse

pistachio salt to rim the glass (see method)
50 ml (1⅔ fl oz) Herradura Reposado tequila
25 ml (¾ fl oz) fresh lime juice
10 ml (⅓ fl oz) vanilla syrup
1 barspoon fig jam

To make the pistachio salt, blend a
few pistachio nuts in a hard spice
grinder and add salt to taste.

To make the cocktail, rim a coupette
glass with the pistachio salt. Shake the
remaining ingredients with ice and fine-
strain into the glass.

Coupette

George's Julep

30 ml (1 fl oz) peach shrub
  (see method)
45 ml (1½ fl oz) Pisco
6–8 mint leaves
dash of peach bitters
mint sprig to garnish

To make the peach shrub, in a saucepan over low heat, gently warm 250 g (9 oz/2 cups) peach purée, 440 g (15½ oz/2 cups) sugar and 250 ml (8½ fl oz/1 cup) apple cider vinegar until the sugar dissolves. Remove from the heat and leave to cool.

Build the cocktail in a highball glass with crushed ice and swizzle. Garnish with a mint sprig.

Highball

Death Flip

30 ml (1 fl oz) quality blanco tequila
15 ml (½ fl oz) Jägermeister
15 ml (½ fl oz) yellow Chartreuse
dash of gomme syrup
1 egg
freshly grated nutmeg to garnish

Dry-shake all the ingredients. Shake with ice and fine-strain into a Champagne flute. Garnish with the nutmeg.

Champagne flute

Foreign Legion

45 ml (1½ fl oz) Ron Zacapa Centenario
   23-year-old rum
15 ml (½ fl oz) Aperol
15 ml (½ fl oz) Dubonnet
15 ml (½ fl oz) Manzanilla dry sherry
5 ml (¼ fl oz) dark crème de cacao
dash of Fee Brothers Rhubarb Bitters
orange twist to garnish

Stir all the ingredients with a chunk of
ice in an old-fashioned glass. Garnish
with an orange twist.

Old-fashioned

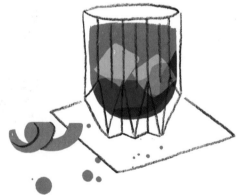

Florodora Imperial Style

30 ml (1 fl oz) cognac
15 ml (½ fl oz) fresh lime juice
15 ml (½ fl oz) raspberry syrup
45 ml (1½ fl oz) Champagne
mint sprig to garnish

Build all the ingredients in an old-fashioned glass with
ice cubes. Garnish with a mint sprig.

Old-fashioned

Thompson & Thomson

45 ml (1½ fl oz) Broker's gin
15 ml (½ fl oz) St Germain elderflower liqueur
15 ml (½ fl oz) sugar and lemongrass syrup
  (1:1 sugar syrup and lemongrass syrup)
25 ml (¾ fl oz) fresh lemon juice
2 dashes of orange blossom water
1 slice cucumber

Shake all the ingredients with ice and fine-strain into a coupette
glass. Garnish with a cucumber slice.

Coupette

Zombie

30 ml (1 fl oz) fresh pineapple juice
30 ml (1 fl oz) fresh orange juice
15 ml (½ fl oz) apricot brandy
1 tablespoon sugar
60 ml (2 fl oz/¼ cup) white rum
30 ml (1 fl oz) dark rum
30 ml (1 fl oz) fresh lime juice
15 ml (½ fl oz) Bacardi 151 rum
slice of fruit, a mint sprig and a
    maraschino cherry to garnish

Mix all the ingredients with ice, except
the Bacardi 151 rum and garnishes. Pour
into a collins glass. Float the Bacardi on
top. Garnish with the fruit slice, sprig of
mint and maraschino cherry.

Collins

Eleventh Hour Julep

50 ml (1⅔ fl oz) Maker's Mark bourbon
2 barspoons orgeat syrup
2 barspoons pomegranate molasses
dash of Peychaud's bitters
mint sprig and 3 skewered craisins to garnish

Build the cocktail in a julep cup over crushed ice.
Garnish with the mint sprig and skewered craisins.

Julep cup

The Andrijich Cocktail

50 ml (1⅔ fl oz) Pisco
25 ml (¾ fl oz) fresh lemon juice
10 ml (⅓ fl oz) sugar syrup (see page 9)
1 barspoon absinthe
dash of egg white
apple cider
rose petal to garnish

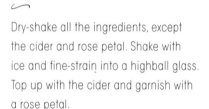

Dry-shake all the ingredients, except
the cider and rose petal. Shake with
ice and fine-strain into a highball glass.
Top up with the cider and garnish with
a rose petal.

Highball

Perfect Serve

60 ml (2 fl oz/¼ cup) San Cosme mezcal
slice of orange and worm salt to garnish

Add the mezcal to a shot glass and
garnish with a slice of orange and
worm salt.

Shot

Kir Royale

30 ml (1 fl oz) crème de cassis
Champagne
lemon twist to garnish

Add the crème de cassis to a Champagne flute and
top with Champagne. Garnish with a lemon twist.

Champagne

Rags to Riches

20 ml (⅔ fl oz) sangria syrup (see method)
40 ml (1⅓ fl oz) Woodford Reserve bourbon
20 ml (⅔ fl oz) chocolate liqueur
20 ml (⅔ fl oz) fresh lemon juice
3 Griottines cherries to garnish

To make the sangria syrup, muddle 1 quartered orange and 10 maraschino cherries and place them with 2 cinnamon sticks and 5 star anise in a glass or plastic jar. Add 750 ml (25½ fl oz/3 cups) Shiraz or Cabernet wine and shake. Leave to sit for 1 week. Strain off the solids and stir in 1 kg (2 lb 3 oz) sugar to make a syrup. Allow to cool. This will keep for 2 weeks in the refrigerator.

To make the cocktail, shake all the ingredients with ice. Double-strain into a chilled coupette glass. Garnish with three Griottines cherries on a skewer.

Coupette

Manhattan

135 g (5 oz/1 cup) ice cubes
15 ml (½ fl oz) sweet vermouth
60 ml (2 fl oz/¼ cup) Irish whiskey
1 dash of bitters
1 maraschino cherry

Place the ice in a mixing glass. Pour in the
vermouth and whiskey and stir. Strain into a martini
glass. Add a dash of bitters and garnish with a
maraschino cherry. To make a dry Manhattan, use
dry vermouth instead.

Martini

Georgetown Swizzle

8–10 mint leaves
1 barspoon sugar
60 ml (2 fl oz/¼ cup) Rémy Martin VSOP cognac
dash of peach bitters
15 ml (½ fl oz) peach and ginger shrub (see method)
mint sprig to garnish

To make the peach and ginger shrub, add 500 g (1 lb 2 oz) sectioned, ripe peaches and 100 g (3½ oz) peeled and chopped fresh ginger to a jar and muddle. Pour in 750 ml (25½ fl oz/3 cups) apple cider vinegar and let sit for 24 hours. Strain off the solids and heat the liquid in a saucepan on the stovetop, but do not boil. Add 1 kg (2 lb 3 oz) sugar and stir to dissolve. Allow to cool. This will keep for 2 weeks in the refrigerator.

To make the cocktail, add the mint leaves to a julep cup and place the sugar on top. Press with the back of the barspoon (careful not to tear or crush the mint) to release the oils into the sugar. Add the cognac, bitters and shrub. Stir with crushed ice until frosted. Top with more crushed ice and garnish with a mint sprig.

Julep cup

Pink Fox

45 ml (1½ fl oz) Beefeater gin
15 ml (½ fl oz) Disaronno amaretto
15 ml (½ fl oz) Crawley's Bartender
   orgeat syrup
5 ml (¼ fl oz) Massenez grenadine
pulp of 1 passionfruit
30 ml (1 fl oz) fresh lemon juice
1 egg white
dash of soda water (club soda)

Add all the ingredients, except the soda water, to a shaker and shake without ice. Add ice and shake, then strain into a chilled Champagne flute. Dash with soda water to create a fluffy head.

Champagne

Coco 'n' Oil

60 ml (2 fl oz/¼ cup) dark rum
10 ml (⅓ fl oz) John D. Taylor's
   Velvet Falernum
10 ml (⅓ fl oz) fresh lime juice
dash of bitters
100 ml (3½ fl oz) coconut water with
   1 egg white added

Add all the ingredients, except the coconut mixture, to a mixing glass and stir down until chilled and diluted. Strain over ice into a whisky glass. Dry-shake the coconut water and egg white, and spoon the foam on top of the drink.

Whisky

Mezcalicious

30 ml (1 fl oz) San Cosme mezcal
15 ml (½ fl oz) Cointreau
30 ml (1 fl oz) fresh orange juice
5 ml (¼ fl oz) fresh lime juice
worm salt to garnish

Shake all the ingredients with ice and
fine-strain into a chilled martini glass.
Garnish with worm salt.

Martini

Benja Collins

50 ml (1⅔ fl oz) San Cosme mezcal
25 ml (¾ fl oz) fresh orange juice
12.5 ml (⅓ fl oz) sugar syrup (see page 9)
soda water (club soda)
orange slice to garnish

Shake the mezcal, orange juice and syrup with ice
and strain into an ice-filled collins glass. Top up
with soda water and garnish with an orange slice.

Collins

Chacalco

10 ml (⅓ fl oz) fresh lime juice
2 lime wedges
50 ml (1⅔ fl oz) San Cosme mezcal
3 pinches of salt
cola

Add the lime juice to a collins glass.
Rub a lime wedge around the rim of the
glass. Fill the collins glass with ice and
add the mezcal and salt. Top with cola
and stir. Garnish with the remaining
lime wedge.

Collins

Kumquat Mojito

2 kumquats
5 mint leaves
2 lime wedges
1½ tablespoons sugar
90 ml (3 fl oz) white rum
splash of Cointreau

Slice the kumquats and add to a mixing
glass with the mint leaves, lime wedges
and sugar. Muddle and then add ice,
rum and Cointreau and shake. Serve in
a highball glass.

Highball

Pink Squirrel

45 ml (1½ fl oz) crème de noyaux
45 ml (1½ fl oz) crème de cacao
15 ml (½ fl oz) vodka
30 ml (1 fl oz) pouring (single/light)
 cream

Pour all the ingredients over
ice in a mixing glass. Stir and
strain into a martini glass.

Martini

The Condoleeza

45 ml (1½ fl oz) Havana Club 3-year-old rum
60 ml (2 fl oz/¼ cup) horchata (Mexican rice water –
   see method)
10 ml (⅓ fl oz) fresh lime juice
40 ml (1⅓ fl oz) orgeat syrup
40 ml (1⅓ fl oz) Fernet-Branca liqueur
mint sprig and lime slice to garnish

To make the horchata, blend 200 g (7 oz/1 cup)
rice with 2 cinnamon sticks. Pour into a large bowl
and steep this mixture in 500 ml (17 fl oz/2 cups)
water for 1 hour. Strain the liquid into a bowl, using
a piece of muslin (cheesecloth). Stir through 110 g
(4 oz/½ cup) sugar and 750 ml (25½ fl oz/3 cups)
water and set aside. Use within a week.

To make the cocktail, build all the ingredients in a
highball glass and swizzle with crushed ice. Garnish
with a mint sprig and a lime slice.

Highball

Gringo's Grange

45 ml (1½ fl oz) Herradura Reposado tequila
40 ml (1⅓ fl oz) apple juice
20 ml (¾ fl oz) Australian Shiraz
15 ml (½ fl oz) agave nectar
10 ml (⅓ fl oz) fresh lemon juice
thin slice of orange and a cinnamon stick to garnish

Heat all the ingredients in a saucepan over low
heat. Pour into a jam jar and garnish with a
thin orange slice and a cinnamon stick.

Jam jar

The Cocktail Dress Girl

The cocktail dress girl begins her day as the sun goes down. As the peachy sunset kicks in, her favourite outfits come out to play and evening cocktails rule her sway. She's the one who arrives fashionably but never late, is the spirited socialite at A-list parties and saves her fancy gowns for late-night soirees. Always sophisticated and elegant, the cocktail dress girl is chic with an eye on luxurious georgette silk dresses and crepe de chine in her desire for everlasting luxury. At times there are beads and sequins, and occasionally plunging necklines and ruffled layers; but she's always magically groomed with a heart that beats for glamour.

When she charges her glass she'll drink those cocktails that come in shades of her favourite dresses – from syrupy peach to Limoncello yellow and the occasional metallic shimmer. And when it comes to dressing her taste buds, she'll rendezvous with classics and embrace modern takes on those that have come before because they tick with a here-and-now spirit.

The cocktail dress girl is always ready to celebrate and lives for the cocktail hour. She thanks Christian Dior for inventing the term 'cocktail dress' as a means to describe the sumptuous early evening wear that she lives by.

Mandarin Beauty

45 ml (1½ fl oz) vodka
15 ml (½ fl oz) Chambord
30 ml (1 fl oz) sweet-and-sour mix
edible flower to garnish

Shake all the ingredients with ice
and strain into an old-fashioned glass.
Garnish with an edible flower.

Old-fashioned

Ciao Bella

45 ml (1½ fl oz) amaretto
20 ml (⅔ fl oz) strawberry liqueur
30 ml (1 fl oz) fresh lemon juice
5 ml (¼ fl oz) sugar syrup (see page 9)
dash of egg white

Shake all the ingredients with ice and double-strain into a martini glass.

Martini

Next Generation

45 ml (1½ fl oz) Sauza Tres Generaciones Añejo tequila
30 ml (1 fl oz) apple juice
15 ml (½ fl oz) fresh lime juice
10 ml (⅓ fl oz) crème de cassis
10 ml (⅓ fl oz) falernum
apple fan to garnish (see page 47)

Shake all the ingredients with ice and strain
into a martini glass. Garnish with an apple fan.

Martini

Shanghai Tan

60 ml (2 fl oz/¼ cup) white rum
30 ml (1 fl oz) anisette syrup, plus a dash
  extra to finish
30 ml (1 fl oz) fresh lemon juice
2 drops of bitters

Shake all the ingredients with ice. Strain into
a martini glass. Finish with a dash of anisette
to float.

Martini

Thujone Cocktail

20 ml (⅔ fl oz) juniper-infused absinthe
  (see method)
30 ml (1 fl oz) dry vermouth
30 ml (1 fl oz) fresh lime juice
3 sage leaves
3 barspoons caster (superfine) sugar
15 ml (½ fl oz) egg white

To make the juniper-infused absinthe,
add 15 g (½ oz) dried juniper to a
bottle of absinthe. Agitate daily for
a week, then strain out the juniper.

To make the cocktail, add all the
ingredients to a cocktail shaker and
shake briefly without ice. Add ice, shake
and double-strain into a coupette glass.

Coupette

Mata Hari

60 ml (2 fl oz/¼ cup) vodka
15 ml (½ fl oz) cranberry juice
juice of ½ lime
lemon twist to garnish

Shake all the ingredients with ice and
pour into a martini glass. Garnish with
a lemon twist.

Martini

Black Caviar

30 ml (1 fl oz) Belvedere vodka
30 ml (1 fl oz) Patrón XO Cafe
30 ml (1 fl oz) fresh espresso coffee
10 ml (⅓ fl oz) agave nectar
clover leaf to garnish

Shake all the ingredients with ice then
double-strain into a martini glass.
Garnish with a clover leaf.

Martini

Aiko Flower

45 ml (1½ fl oz) TK 40 sake
15 ml (½ fl oz) crème de pêche
15 ml (½ fl oz) crème de violette
15 ml (½ fl oz) cranberry juice
wedge of lime
Luxardo maraschino cherry to garnish

Add all the ingredients, except the lime and cherry, to a shaker, shake vigorously with ice and double-strain into a martini glass. Squeeze the lime on top. Garnish with a Luxardo maraschino cherry.

Martini

Blue Eyes

80 g (2¾ oz/½ cup) blueberries
60 ml (2 fl oz/¼ cup) pineapple juice
25 ml (¾ fl oz) fresh lime juice
15 ml (½ fl oz) sugar syrup (see page 9)
lime twist and 2 blueberries to garnish

Process all the ingredients, except the garnish, in a blender with ice until smooth. Pour into a poco glass and garnish with a lime twist and 2 blueberries.

Poco

Long Jing Mar-Tea-Ni

60 ml (2 fl oz/¼ cup) vodka
30 ml (1 fl oz) Long Jing green tea syrup
Long Jin tea leaves to garnish

Stir the vodka and green tea syrup with ice and strain into a martini glass. Garnish with Long Jing tea leaves.

Martini

Sidecar

45 ml (1½ fl oz) cognac or brandy
30 ml (1 fl oz) Cointreau
15 ml (½ fl oz) fresh lemon juice
lemon twist to garnish

Pour all the ingredients into a cocktail
shaker with ice. Shake well and serve
in a martini glass. Garnish with a
lemon twist.

Martini

Gin Sling

45 ml (1½ fl oz) gin
30 ml (1 fl oz) sweet vermouth
30 ml (1 fl oz) sugar syrup (see page 9)
dash of angostura bitters
soda water (club soda)
lemon twist to garnish

Pour all the ingredients, except the soda
water, in a shaker filled with ice. Shake
well. Strain into a chilled collins glass
and top with soda water. Garnish with a
lemon twist.

Collins

Amanigai Symphony

15 ml (½ fl oz) egg white
30 ml (1 fl oz) Belvedere vodka
30 ml (1 fl oz) peach schnapps
30 ml (1 fl oz) Campari
15 ml (½ fl oz) yuzu juice
15 ml (½ fl oz) fresh lemon juice
15 ml (½ fl oz) sugar syrup (see page 9)
grapefruit twist to garnish

Dry-shake the egg white, add the other
ingredients, shake and strain into a short martini
glass with ice. Garnish with a grapefruit twist.

Short martini

Black Russian

45 ml (1½ fl oz) vodka
25 ml (¾ fl oz) coffee liqueur

Build the cocktail in an old-fashioned
glass filled with ice. Stir well.

Old-fashioned

VODKA

Mayan Sacrifice

30 ml (1 fl oz) Ron Zacapa Centenario
  23-year-old rum
25 ml (¾ fl oz) Cinzano Rosso
15 ml (½ fl oz) Heering cherry liqueur
20 ml (⅔ fl oz) blood plum–infused Tokay (see method)
grapefruit twist to garnish

To make the blood plum–infused Tokay, soak
3 peeled and chopped blood plums in a bottle
of Tokay, and allow to sit until ready to use.

To make the cocktail, combine all the
ingredients in a mixing glass with ice and stir.
Strain into a martini glass and garnish with a
grapefruit twist.

Martini

David's Sour

30 ml (1 fl oz) dark rum
15 ml (½ fl oz) Cointreau
15 ml (½ fl oz) fresh lemon juice
sparkling wine

Pour the rum, Cointreau and lemon juice
into a highball glass with ice. Top up with
sparkling wine.

Highball

Cosmopolitan

60 ml (2 fl oz/¼ cup) vodka
30 ml (1 fl oz) Cointreau
1 teaspoon fresh lime juice
125 ml (4 fl oz/½ cup) cranberry juice

Place ice in a martini glass. Shake
the vodka, Cointreau and lime and
cranberry juices with ice. Strain into
the prepared glass and serve.

Martini

Sakura

30 ml (1 fl oz) Japanese single malt whisky
15 ml (½ fl oz) Heering cherry liqueur
10 ml (⅓ fl oz) Pedro Ximénez sherry
2 dashes of aromatic bitters
fresh cherry to garnish

Add all the ingredients to a mixing glass
with ice. Stir and strain into a coupette
glass. Garnish with a fresh cherry.

Coupette

Sin City Rodriguez

45 ml (1½ fl oz) Ilegal Mezcal Joven tequila
1 tablespoon apricot and rhubarb jam
90 ml (3 fl oz) raspberry juice
small splash of fresh lime juice

Shake all the ingredients and serve in a martini glass with 1 ice cube.

Martini

The Rum Revolva

30 ml (1 fl oz) maple syrup and cardamom pod reduction (see method)
45 ml (1½ fl oz) Appleton Estate V/X rum
30 ml (1 fl oz) Joseph Cartron white liqueur de cacao
6 sage leaves
orange twist and 2 pineapple leaves to garnish

To make the maple syrup and cardamom reduction, add 20 cardamom pods to 500 ml (17 fl oz/2 cups) maple syrup and 500 ml (17 fl oz/2 cups) water. Heat on a stovetop over low heat until reduced by half. Strain out the cardamom pods and leave to cool.

Add all the ingredients to a shaker. Shake vigorously with ice and strain into a highball glass over crushed ice. Garnish with an orange twist and 2 pineapple leaves.

Highball

Smoking Guns

3 sage leaves
45 ml (1½ fl oz) Ilegal Mezcal Joven tequila
30 ml (1 fl oz) fresh lemon juice
15 ml (½ fl oz) yellow Chartreuse
25 ml (¾ fl oz) sugar syrup (see page 9)
5 dashes of Bittermens Hellfire Habanero Shrub bitters
1 stemmed sage leaf to garnish

Lightly muddle the sage leaves in a Boston shaker then add the other ingredients. Add ice, shake and double-strain into a coupette glass. Garnish with the stemmed sage leaf.

Coupette

Fresh Passionfruit Shooter

1 passionfruit
15 ml (½ fl oz) triple sec
60 ml (2 fl oz/¼ cup) Absolut Kurant vodka
splash of fresh lime juice

Cut the passionfruit in half and shuck it like
an oyster, leaving the fruit inside the shell.
(This makes 2 shots – one for each passionfruit half.)
In a shaker of ice add all the other ingredients and
shake to oblivion, then strain into each half
shell and shoot.

Passionfruit shell

French Shiso Sour

60 ml (2 fl oz/¼ cup) Hennessy VS cognac
45 ml (1½ fl oz) fresh lemon juice
4 dashes of Jerry Thomas bitters or
   angostura bitters, plus extra to serve
10 ml (⅓ fl oz) sugar syrup (see page 9)
4 shiso or basil leaves
1 egg white
1 shiso leaf to garnish

Add all the ingredients to a mixing glass and
process with a stick blender. If you don't have a
stick blender you can shake in your chosen shaker.
After the liquid is combined and the egg white
fluffy, pour into your shaker, add ice and shake
vigorously for 15–20 seconds. Double-strain into a
coupette glass, making sure you catch all the flecks
of shiso leaf in your strainer. Garnish with a shiso
leaf on the edge of the glass and a few drops of
bitters for aroma.

Coupette

Number 6

4 Vietnamese mint leaves, plus extra to garnish
60 ml (2 fl oz/¼ cup) Havana Club Blanco rum
30 ml (1 fl oz) Choya plum wine
20 ml (⅔ fl oz) chilli and passionfruit syrup
   (see method)
20 ml (⅔ fl oz) fresh lime juice
soda water (club soda)

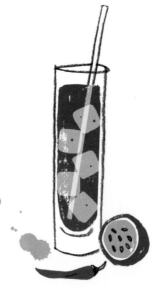

To make the chilli and passionfruit syrup, bring
1 litre (34 fl oz/4 cups) water to the boil,
add 1.25 kg (2 lb 12 oz) sugar and stir until
dissolved. Add 12–15 bird's eye chillies and
500 ml (17 fl oz/2 cups) tinned passionfruit
pulp. Reduce until you have a syrup-like
consistency. Fine-strain. Cool before using.

To make the cocktail, bruise the mint leaves and
drop them into the bottom of a highball glass.
Add ice and build the cocktail like a mojito. Top
with crushed ice and then top up with soda
water. Garnish with the extra Vietnamese mint.

Highball

Undertow 16

45 ml (1½ fl oz) 42 Below Feijoa vodka
20 ml (⅔ fl oz) fresh lime juice
40 ml (1⅓ fl oz) fresh ruby grapefruit juice
tonic water
rosemary sprig to garnish

Build the cocktail in a highball glass with ice
and top with tonic water. Garnish with a sprig
of rosemary.

Highball

Lychee Martini

30 ml (1 fl oz) lychee liqueur
30 ml (1 fl oz) vanilla vodka
lychee to garnish

Stir the lychee liqueur and vodka with ice and strain into a martini glass. Garnish with a lychee.

Martini

The Byzantine

30 ml (1 fl oz) Aperol
30 ml (1 fl oz) Finlandia grapefruit vodka
30 ml (1 fl oz) fresh lemon juice
dash of pomegranate molasses
dash of Fee Brothers Rhubarb Bitters
1 egg white
grapefruit twist to garnish

Shake all the ingredients and pour into an old-fashioned glass with ice. Garnish with a grapefruit twist.

Old-fashioned

The Cocktail Dress Girl 201

Index

Acknowledgements

IN MEMORY OF Motor City Bar, NYC

The fabulous cocktails you find in this book are kindly donated by some of Melbourne's, Sydney's and New York's best bartenders. Without them this book would not have been possible. I highly recommend you explore their cocktail lists and indulge (when you're not making them at home of course).

Albert Park Hotel; Atrium Bar, Crown Melbourne; Bill's Bar, Fitzroy (Dante Ruaine and Naomi Clarks); Black Pearl, Fitzroy (Chris Hysted); Brooks Bar (Shae Silvestro); Captain Melville, Melbourne (Jason Crawley); Cellar Bar, St Kilda; Circa, The Prince; Claremont Tonic, South Yarra; Coda (James Tait and Mykal Bartholemew); Comme, Melbourne; David's Restaurant, Prahran; duNord Bar, Melbourne (Thomas Kiltorp and Sam Friend); Eau De Vie, Melbourne (Greg Sanderson, Jamie Chesher, Josh Crawford and Claire Wong); Gilt Lounge QT, Sydney; Hobba Eatery & Bar, Prahran; Joe's Bar & Dining Hall, St Kilda; Livingroom Restaurant, Malvern; Morris Jones Bar & Restaurant, Windsor; Motor City Bar New York (Jodi Ham); Mr Hive Kitchen & Bar, Crown Melbourne; Newmarket Hotel, St Kilda; Nobu, Crown Melbourne; Otto's Shrunken Head, New York; Pawn & Co, South Yarra (Joel Heffernan); Rockpool Bar & Grill, Melbourne; Rosetta, Crown Melbourne (Paul Hammond); Royal Saxon, Richmond; Saké Restaurant and Bar, Melbourne; Silks, Crown Melbourne; Spice Temple, Melbourne; Stokehouse Café, St Kilda; Stokehouse Restaurant, St Kilda; The Breslin Bar & Grill, Melbourne; The Point Restaurant, Albert Park; Tio's Cerveceria, Sydney (Jeremy Blackmore); The Aylesbury, Melbourne; The Den @ The Atlantic, Crown Melbourne; The Everleigh, Fitzroy; The Merrywell, Crown Melbourne; The Smith Restaurant & Bar, Prahran; The Spice Market, Melbourne; The Waiting Room, Crown Melbourne; The Water Bar Sydney (Black PR group); Touche Hombre, Melbourne; Transit Cocktail Lounge, Federation Square, Melbourne; Trocadero, Melbourne; Understudy, Melbourne; Waterbar @ Blue, Sydney; 1806, Melbourne.

People To Thank

My beautiful partner, Robert McMahon and our daughter, Sunny Rose; my parents Clara and Frank Rocca; my grandparents Emilio and Rosa D'Ambrosio; big love to the ladies who turn frocks to 11 – Mishell Vreman, Mel Ogier, Isabel Pappani, Johanna Greenway, Emma Brady, Emilia Toia and Mary Mihelakos; Eileen Berry @ *The Weekly Review*; a special thanks and big bundle of love to Tara Bishop and Crown Melbourne; Clemence Harvey and Liz Fry @ Harvey Publicity; Dean Lucas and Sebastian Reaburn from 666, Pure Tasmanian Vodka, Pure Distillery Company; Jenny Brookes from The Melbourne Pub Group; Matt Vines @ EVH PR; Hayden Burbank @ Morris Jones Bar & Restaurant; a massive thanks to the ever so lovely Chris Hysted @ Black Pearl who came to the rescue many times; Mr Mexico's Creative Director Ricardo Amare; Pru Corrigan @ Two Birds Talking; Michael Madrusan @ The Everleigh; Susie Robinson @ PR Darling; Kate Keane and her fabulous team at Kate & Co; a special thanks to the lovely Jannah Flockhart; Annabelle Jones and Abbey Thomas @ AMPR; Michelle Campbell @ Minc; my beautiful J-Bird sister in New York – Jodi Ham who got me addicted to fancy cocktails more than 10 years ago; Sam Dennis and Mick Formosa – Belvedere Brand Ambassadors; Fiona Brook and Mia Cochrane @ Zilla & Brook PR; Hot House Media & Events – John Flower and Terese Nguyen; Helen Reizer; Jason Williams – Group Bars Manager, The Keystone Group Sydney – for his commitment to help out with my book a second time round; Greg Sanderson; Shae Silvestro; Dante Ruaine; the gorgeous gal Danica Sladic; Ellie MacDiarmid; Sarah Seddon and Nicole Haddow from The Atlantic Group; David Bloustein, Jarritos Australasia; San Pellegrino; Ketel One Vodka; Ultimat Vodka; The Mint Partners; and The Van Handeel family; had lots of fun giving my Magimix Chrome Blender a good workout too – thanks to AMPR for their help with this one; to the fabulous NYC Motor City Bar and Otto's Shrunken Head – thanks for your support. To my editors Lucy Heaver and Ariana Klepac, publisher Paul McNally and fabulous illustrator Neryl Walker – she has amazing style. And of course, Pierre Baroni, the original soul brother – and the only man I trust with a camera. Now stop reading the credits, thanks, and start drinking, goddamn!

Published in 2013 by Hardie Grant Books

Hardie Grant Books (Australia)
Ground Floor, Building 1
658 Church Street
Richmond, Victoria 3121
www.hardiegrant.com.au

Hardie Grant Books (UK)
Dudley House, North Suite
34–35 Southampton Street
London WC2E 7HF
www.hardiegrant.co.uk

A Cataloguing-in-Publication entry is available from the catalogue of the National Library of Australia at www.nla.gov.au

The Fashionable Cocktail

9781742706139

Publishing Director: Paul McNally
Managing Editor: Lucy Heaver
Editor: Ariana Klepac
Design Manager: Heather Menzies
Design Assistant: Aileen Lord
Illustrator: Neryl Walker
Production Manager: Todd Rechner

Colour reproduction by Splitting Image Colour Studio

Printed in China by 1010 Printing International Limited